BACK TO SCHOOL

BEETLEJUICE

BIG NIGHT

BREAKFAST AT TIFFANY'S

EAT DRINK MAN WOMAN

ELF

THE GOLD RUSH

GOODFELLAS

INGLOURIOUS BASTERDS

JULIE & JULIA

KRAMER VS. KRAMER

MOONLIGHT

RATATOUILLE

ROMAN HOLIDAY

SABRINA

SATURDAY NIGHT FEVER

UNCLE BUCK

WHAT ABOUT BOB?

WHEN HARRY MET SALLY...

WHIPLASH

EAT WHAT YOU WATCH

EAT WHAT YOU WATCH

A COOKBOOK FOR MOVIE LOVERS

ANDREW REA

PHOTOGRAPHY BY
SCOTT GORDON BLEICHER

DOVETAIL

NEW YORK

For the one who taught me how to cook,
taught me how to live, taught me
how to love—my mother.

CONTENTS

INTRODUCTION

Food in movies and television plays just as vital and important a role as any of the human characters. It gets a styling of its own and is crucial in bringing stories together; it's present during pivotal scenes to communicate emotion; it serves in framing place, time and the general zeitgeist; and it ingrains itself in the viewer's memory forever.

I, for one, can't remember the names of my best friends from elementary school, but from that same era, I can vividly remember the abandoned jellies and cakes in the lobby scene of *Jurassic Park*. And the feast of takeout hurriedly plated (and taken credit for) by Mrs. Doubtfire after she sets fire to her blouse. And the platter of delicious finger food extolled by Lumiere in *Beauty and the Beast*. And the neon-colored pies flung across the table in *Hook*. (As a matter of fact, that's about all I can remember from that movie.) I'm willing to bet that you, too, harbor some movie-food memories from childhood, be it Kronk's spinach puffs from *The Emperor's New Groove* or E.T.'s Reese's Pieces. The foods we see on screen stay with us—and we crave them forever.

It's no surprise, then, that we often want to eat what we see on screen. We can't help but associate the food with the characters and their lives. In fact, food in movies and television is a powerful form of subliminal advertising.

Almost two decades after *Sex and the City* debuted, lines at New York City's Magnolia Bakery still snake out the door thanks to the cupcake shop's prominence in an episode of the TV show. Katz's Delicatessen has a wooden plaque commemorating the famous "orgasm" scene from *When Harry Met Sally . . .* (page 86). Seabass was nearly fished into extinction after its mere mention by Richard Attenborough's character in *Jurassic Park*. Patrons at the Wizarding World of Harry Potter in Orlando reportedly cried upon taking their first sip of Butterbeer (page 34). It's the food of fiction made tangible, confections seemingly out of reach now available at a location near you.

Food and movies are both sources of diversion, comfort and togetherness, and they constantly inspire one another. They inspired me back in 2016 to create *Binging with Babish*, a web series in which I try to accurately recreate the foods of film and television. I had always been curious about the foods of fiction, and unwittingly spent my entire life cultivating a deep-seated love of both cinema and cuisine. When the two almost accidentally came together in my kitchen, I knew that I had found my calling. Energized by the tantalizing cross-section of passion and play, I'd come home almost every night after work and experiment in the kitchen late into the night, leaving a trail of dirty dishes and ruined aprons behind me. The effort has paid off: *Binging with Babish* has become my full-time job, has introduced me to a host of new experiences and people (including the love of my life), and at the time of this writing, has garnered more than 40 million views. It seems that many others share the same passion for food on film as I do, and it's a continuing joy to share with them the creativity, spontaneity, and fantasy that goes along with it.

This book is all about bringing that delicious fiction to life and manifesting our food fantasies in our very own kitchens. Cooking these recipes is one of the most accessible ways to experience firsthand what the characters are seeing, smelling, and tasting. There's something undeniably special about cutting into your first *Big Night* Timpano (page 106) and seeing the layers stacked with wild Italian abandon. Some recipes are offerings of exhaustive accuracy, such as the Confit Byaldi from *Ratatouille* (page 52), while others are spiritual homages to their source material, like the French Toast from *Kramer vs. Kramer* (page 26). No matter which dishes you try for yourself, I hope they help you bring your favorite movies to life.

★ ANGEL FOOD CAKE ★

In one of the most surprisingly "phil"-osophical comedies ever made, Bill Murray portrays a conceited and self-centered weatherman stuck in an endless time loop, reliving the same day over and over. As inconvenient as that sounds, the plot also allows him to indulge in things without consequences. In an iconic scene of ultimate gluttony, he gorges himself on a beautiful breakfast in Punxsutawney's Tip Top Café, where he shoves a whole angel food cake in his mouth, much to Andie MacDowell's character's disgust. You may be tempted to do the same thing with a nice piece of this iteration, but remember, you will have to live with the shame and guilt tomorrow.

Ingredients   *Makes 1 cake (about 12 servings)*

12 egg whites, at room temperature

½ teaspoon pure vanilla extract

½ teaspoon fresh lemon juice

1½ teaspoons cream of tartar

1½ cups cake flour

1½ cups superfine sugar

½ teaspoon kosher salt

1 cup heavy cream

¼ cup granulated sugar

2 cups strawberries, hulled and quartered

Preheat the oven to 350°.

In the bowl of a stand mixer fitted with a whisk attachment, combine the egg whites, vanilla, lemon juice and cream of tartar. Beat at medium-high speed until the egg whites hold medium to stiff peaks.

In a bowl, sift together the flour, superfine sugar and salt. Sift a small amount of the flour mixture over the egg whites and fold gently with a rubber spatula. Continue to fold in the rest of the dry ingredients, taking care not to deflate the egg whites. Once the batter has been combined, pour it into an ungreased tube pan with a removable bottom, spreading the batter evenly with a rubber spatula. Place the pan in the oven and bake for 30 to 40 minutes, or until a toothpick inserted into the center of the cake comes out clean. Place the pan upside down on a wire rack and let cool for at least 1 hour and 30 minutes before removing the pan. (If your tube pan doesn't have feet, suspend the pan on a wine bottle.)

While the cake cools, combine the cream and 2 tablespoons of the granulated sugar in the bowl of the stand mixer and beat at medium speed until soft peaks form. Refrigerate until ready to serve.

In a small bowl, combine the strawberries with the remaining 2 tablespoons of granulated sugar. Let the berries sit for at least 10 minutes.

Once the cake has cooled completely, run a long knife around the edge of the pan to loosen the cake. Place the cake, right side up, on a cake stand or serving plate. Slice the cake, top with the whipped cream and strawberries and serve.

Rita: "Don't you worry about cholesterol, lung cancer, love handles?"

Phil: "I don't worry about anything, anymore... I don't even have to floss."

1993

ASPARAGUS WITH HOLLANDAISE

In an incredibly tense dinner scene in Sam Mendes's directorial debut, *American Beauty*, a family's roiling tensions come to a head over a plate of un-passed asparagus. Lester Burnham, the patriarch played by Kevin Spacey, then theatrically gets up from the table and hurls the plate at the wall, making the poor asparagus collateral damage on his new path of not giving a bleep anymore. Here is a redeeming version of this dish with a rich hollandaise sauce and a luxuriously runny egg—please pass gently.

Ingredients   *Makes 4 servings*

1 whole egg plus 4 large egg yolks

3 tablespoons fresh lemon juice

½ teaspoon kosher salt

¼ teaspoon cayenne pepper

½ cup (1 stick) unsalted butter, melted

1 tablespoon white wine vinegar

1 bay leaf

1 pound asparagus, trimmed

Freshly ground black pepper

Make the hollandaise: In a metal bowl, whisk together 4 egg yolks, 1 tablespoon of the lemon juice, salt and cayenne until combined. In a medium saucepan, bring 1 inch of water to a simmer and place the bowl over the water, making sure the bottom of the bowl doesn't touch the water. Whisk the egg mixture until the yolks are pale yellow and thickened, about 2 minutes. Remove the bowl from the heat. Very slowly drizzle the butter down the side of the bowl, whisking constantly, until the hollandaise becomes thick and creamy, about 1 to 2 minutes.

Poach the egg: Fill a wide saucepan with a few inches of water and bring to a simmer. Add the vinegar. Crack the whole egg into a fine-mesh sieve and swirl to remove the thin liquid around the egg white (this is optional). Swirl a spoon in the boiling water to create a whirlpool. Quickly but gently roll the egg into the simmering water and continue to swirl the water in one direction to help the egg white wrap around itself. Poach the egg until the white is just set and the yolk is still runny, about 3 minutes.

Meanwhile, place the bay leaf and the remaining 2 tablespoons of lemon juice in a large saucepan and fill with enough water to just reach the bottom of a steamer basket. Steam the asparagus until crisp-tender, about 6 to 10 minutes, depending on their size. Transfer the asparagus to a platter or serving dish, top with the hollandaise sauce and the poached egg. Grind some fresh pepper over the top and break the yolk before serving.

"Then I told my boss to go fuck himself, and then I blackmailed him for almost $60,000. Pass the asparagus."
—Lester Burnham

1999

★ BIRTHDAY CAKE ★

This simple-but-delicious layer cake is inspired by the climactic final moments in John Hughes's beloved 1980s Brat Pack–filled flick. Few on-screen foods are as memorable as the birthday cake at the end of *Sixteen Candles*, which is impressive considering that it goes uneaten while two star-crossed teenage protagonists finally get to kiss. This cake is best served as a gesture of affection for the Molly Ringwald in your life.

Ingredients   *Makes 1 cake (about 12 servings)*

For the cake:

2 sticks unsalted butter, softened, plus more for the pans

3 cups cake flour

1 tablespoon baking powder

½ teaspoon baking soda

1 teaspoon kosher salt

1½ cups granulated sugar

2 tablespoons vanilla extract

3 large eggs

1½ cups whole milk

1 cup rainbow sprinkles

For the frosting:

3 sticks unsalted butter, softened

1 tablespoon vanilla extract

5 cups sifted confectioners' sugar

3 tablespoons whole milk

Pink food coloring (or other color of your choice)

Make the cake: Preheat the oven to 350°. Grease two 9-inch cake pans with butter.

In a medium bowl, whisk together the flour, baking powder, baking soda and salt. In the bowl of a stand mixer fitted with a paddle, cream together the butter and the granulated sugar until light and fluffy, then add the vanilla and eggs. With the mixer running at low speed, slowly add the flour mixture and mix until combined. Once the flour mixture has been added, slowly add the milk while the mixer runs. Add the sprinkles and mix until combined.

Pour the batter into the prepared cake pans and bake for 45 to 50 minutes, or until a tester inserted in the center of the cake comes out clean. Invert the cakes onto a wire rack, remove the pans and let cool completely, about 2 hours.

Make the frosting: In the bowl of a stand mixer fitted with a paddle, cream together the butter, vanilla, confectioners' sugar and milk. Transfer about one-fourth of the frosting to a bowl and blend in the food coloring, a small amount at a time, until it's the desired color. Transfer the pink frosting to a pastry bag fitted with the tip of your choice.

If necessary, cut off the domed tops of the individual cakes with a serrated knife. Place a small amount of frosting on the bottom of a cake stand and place the first cake on top. Frost liberally with the white frosting, top with the second cake and repeat. Cover the entire cake with an even layer of frosting and decorate as desired with the piped pink frosting. Cut into slices and serve.

Jake: "Happy birthday, Samantha. Make a wish."

Samantha: "It already came true."

1984

INSPIRED BY

SIXTEEN CANDLES

Chef is, at its core, a film about the virtues of preparing food passionately. And family and whatever. It's got its fair share of cheffy platings and *mmm*-ridden tastings, but it ultimately tells the story of why chef Casper cooks, not what he cooks. Nowhere is this better illustrated than during the first service undertaken by his newly minted food truck, hurriedly assembling Cubanos and lecturing his son about quality control. The motivation and drive behind great food is often what makes it great.

THE CUBANOS

FROM

CHEF

2014

★ BLUEBERRY PIE ★

In Rob Reiner's coming-of-age classic, a gang of boys is on a mission to find a dead body in rural 1950s Oregon. When night falls, they tell stories around the campfire, and Gordie, the leader of the group, recounts the story of a pie-eating contest. Lardass Hogan, a bullied overweight fellow, entered the competition not to win but to exact vomiting revenge on his bullies. What follows is maybe the most revolting vomit sequence in cinema food history. Even that scene, however, won't curb one's desire for homemade blueberry pie with a lard crust, just like they made in rural Oregon. (Do not combine with castor oil.)

Ingredients   *Makes 1 double-crusted pie*

For the crust:

3 cups all-purpose flour, plus more for dusting

2 tablespoons granulated sugar

1 teaspoon kosher salt

10 ounces leaf lard, chilled

⅓ cup ice water, plus more as needed

For the filling:

6 cups fresh or frozen blueberries

½ cup granulated sugar

½ cup cornstarch

½ teaspoon cinnamon

1 whole vanilla bean, split, seeds scraped, or 1 teaspoon pure vanilla extract

Zest and juice of 1 lemon

Salt

For assembly:

1 egg, beaten

1 tablespoon coarse sugar, such as turbinado

"Lardass!
Lardass!
Lardass!"

Make the crust: In a food processor, pulse together the flour, granulated sugar and salt. Cut the lard into ½-inch cubes and add them to the food processor, pulsing until it is cut into pea-size pieces. Transfer the mixture to a large mixing bowl and gradually sprinkle with the ice water while gently folding the dough with a rubber spatula. (Start with ⅓ cup of water and add more as needed until a shaggy dough forms; do not overmix the dough.) Pat the dough into two 1-inch-thick discs, wrap tightly in plastic wrap and refrigerate for at least 2 hours.

While the dough chills, make the filling: In a large bowl, combine the blueberries, granulated sugar, cornstarch, cinnamon, vanilla seeds (or extract), lemon zest, lemon juice and a pinch of salt. Using a rubber spatula, fold the ingredients together until well mixed.

Preheat the oven to 500° and place a rimmed baking sheet on the bottom rack. Remove one dough disc from the refrigerator, unwrap it and place it on a well-floured surface. Using a floured rolling pin, pound the disc down to half its thickness, dusting it with flour as needed. Roll the dough out into an 18-inch round. Transfer the dough by rolling it loosely over the rolling pin and unrolling it into a 9-inch pie pan. Trim the edges of the dough so that it hangs over the pie pan by at least ½ inch. Refrigerate until ready to use.

Pound and roll out the remaining dough into a 16-inch round. Retrieve the prepared pie pan from the refrigerator and fill it with the blueberry mixture, slightly mounding the filling in the center. Using a pastry brush, brush the edges of the bottom crust lightly with water. Top the pie with the second pastry round, pressing around the edges until the crusts are sealed together. Trim the top crust to the same length as the bottom crust and tuck the edges under. Using your fingers (or a fork), crimp a decorative edge around the crust. Cut an X (or other design if desired) into the top of the pie crust for ventilation, and brush liberally with the beaten egg. Sprinkle with the coarse sugar and place in the oven, immediately reducing the temperature to 350°. Bake for 45 to 55 minutes, or until the crust is deeply browned all over. If the edges of the pie begin to get too dark before the rest of the piecrust, wrap them in aluminum foil.

Transfer the pie to a wire rack and let rest for at least 4 hours. Cut and serve (or eat whole without the use of your hands).

1986

★ BOEUF BOURGUIGNON ★

Julie Powell, of the movie *Julie & Julia*, is a food blogger determined to cook through the entirety of Julia Child's classic cookbook *Mastering the Art of French Cooking* in one year. The climax of this feat is her attempt at boeuf bourguignon, a dish so important and representative of the intricacies of traditional French cuisine that she decides to serve it to her first food critic. It's a classic that's hard to improve on, but we've included a pressure cooker version of Ms. Child's signature dish, which saves time without compromising flavor.

Ingredients

Makes 4 servings

2 pounds boneless short ribs (or chuck), cut into 1- to 2-inch cubes

Kosher salt and freshly ground black pepper

5 tablespoons duck fat (or vegetable oil)

2 tablespoons all-purpose flour

2 cups red wine

2 cups water or chicken stock

1 yellow onion, quartered

1 clove, stuck into one of the onion quarters

3 ribs celery, cut into 4-inch pieces

2 rosemary sprigs

4 thyme sprigs

3 garlic cloves, smashed

4 parsley sprigs, plus ¼ cup chopped parsley for garnish

1 teaspoon black peppercorns

2 bay leaves

8 ounces pearl onions, peeled

4 large carrots, peeled and cut into bite-size pieces

8 ounces mushrooms, quartered

2 tablespoons cornstarch (if necessary)

8 ounces dried egg noodles

2 tablespoons unsalted butter

Dry the beef very well with paper towels and season liberally with salt and pepper. In a large Dutch oven, heat 4 tablespoons of the duck fat over medium-high heat. Once it's shimmering, add the beef without overcrowding the pot (leave about 1 inch of room between the pieces). Sear the beef in batches until well browned on two sides. Transfer the meat to a bowl and set aside. When you're finished searing the beef, a deep golden crust should have formed on the bottom of the pot. Sprinkle the flour into the pot and cook over medium heat, whisking constantly, until the flour is lightly browned. Gradually add the red wine, whisking vigorously to break apart any clumps. Once the mixture is smooth, continue cooking until the wine is bubbling and slightly thickened. Remove the pot from the heat.

Pressure cooker method: In a pressure cooker, combine the water or stock, yellow onion (with clove), celery, rosemary, 3 of the thyme sprigs, garlic, the parsley sprigs, peppercorns and bay leaves. Bring to a boil and add the beef and wine mixture. Make sure there's enough liquid to just cover the beef (if not, add more wine). Cover and bring to high pressure for 30 minutes. Release the pressure according to the manufacturer's instructions.

Dutch oven method: To the thickened wine, add the water or stock, yellow onion (with clove), celery, rosemary, 3 of the thyme sprigs, garlic, the parsley sprigs, peppercorns and bay leaves. Make sure there's enough liquid to just cover the beef; if there's not, add more wine. Bring the mixture to a boil, then reduce to a simmer and cover the pot, leaving the lid slightly ajar. Cook until the beef is very tender when pierced with a fork, about 1 hour and 30 minutes.

Preheat the oven to 375° and place a rimmed baking sheet inside. In a large bowl, toss the pearl onions, carrots and mushrooms with the remaining tablespoon of duck fat and leaves from the remaining thyme sprig. Pour the vegetables onto the hot baking sheet and spread them out evenly with a spoon. Roast until tender and browned, about 30 minutes. If the mushrooms start to dry out, remove them from the baking sheet and set aside.

While the vegetables roast, remove the beef from the braising liquid. Strain the liquid through a fine-mesh sieve, pushing on the vegetables with a spoon to extract all the liquid, then discard the braising vegetables. Return the liquid to the pan and bring to a steady simmer. Reduce the liquid until thickened and syrupy. If the mixture doesn't thicken to your liking, blend the cornstarch with ½ cup of cold water, then whisk the cornstarch slurry into the braising liquid, 1 tablespoon at a time, heating gently until thickened. Add the roasted vegetables and beef to the pot.

Cook the egg noodles according to the package directions and drain well. Transfer to a bowl and toss with the butter, then season with salt and pepper. Divide the egg noodles among bowls, ladle the beef stew over the top, garnish with chopped parsley and serve.

2009

BOURBON FRENCH TOAST STICKS

If you're anxiously trying to impress your son in the wake of the dissolution of your marriage and family, or if you just enjoy a good breakfast, you can't go wrong with French toast. Unless, of course, you get eggshells in the batter. Or forget the milk. Or make bread soup. If you're striving for authenticity, try Ted Kramer's eggs-in-a-mug method at home; if you're striving for flavor, take a crack at this bourbon-infused version of the brunch classic.

Ingredients

Makes 2 servings

6 slices brioche, challah or white bread

1 cup whole milk

½ cup heavy cream

¼ cup granulated sugar

4 large eggs

1 teaspoon ground cinnamon

½ teaspoon freshly grated nutmeg

1 teaspoon pure vanilla extract

¼ cup bourbon

3 tablespoons unsalted butter

¼ cup confectioners' sugar

Maple syrup, for serving

Preheat the oven to its lowest setting and cut the brioche slices into 1-inch sticks. Arrange the bread sticks on a baking sheet and bake until mostly dried, about 20 minutes (alternatively, leave the bread out overnight so it becomes stale). Transfer the baking sheet to a wire rack and let the bread cool completely. Leave the oven on, and place a rimmed baking sheet fitted with a wire rack inside.

In a large bowl, whisk together the milk, cream, granulated sugar, eggs, cinnamon, nutmeg, vanilla and bourbon until well mixed. Pour into a dish wide enough for dipping the bread. In a large nonstick pan, heat 1 tablespoon of the butter over medium heat until the foaming subsides. Working with two pieces at a time, dip the bread in the egg mixture until fully coated, let the excess run off, then place in the hot pan. Cook until browned on all sides, then transfer to the baking sheet in the oven to keep warm. Repeat with the remaining bread, adding a tablespoon of butter to the pan before each batch.

Stack the French toast sticks on a plate and use a fine-mesh sieve to dust with confectioners' sugar. Serve with maple syrup.

"What you don't know is that French toast is always folded. You go into the best restaurants anywhere in the world, and you see folded French toast. You get more bites that way, right?"
—Ted Kramer

1979

★ BREAKFAST DESSERT PASTA ★

This high-glycemic dish, concocted by Will Ferrell's character in *Elf*, has a strange allure to it. On the one hand, it's the mishmash of all your favorite childhood treats sprinkled wildly atop a steaming plate of spaghetti. On the other hand, it's absolutely disgusting. Making this pasta might actually be more fun than eating it, but you might surprise yourself when you start shoving it in your mouth with your hands, all hyped up on sugar.

Ingredients

Makes 4 servings

1 pound dried pasta such as spaghetti or linguine

2 tablespoons unsalted butter

½ cup M&Ms

½ cup mini marshmallows

2 fudge Pop-Tarts

¼ cup chocolate syrup

¼ cup caramel sauce

Bring a large pot of salted water to a boil. Add the pasta to the water and cook until al dente. Drain, transfer to a large bowl and toss with the butter.

Divide the pasta among 4 bowls or plates and evenly distribute the M&Ms and mini marshmallows among the servings. Crumble half a Pop-Tart over the top of each serving. Drizzle with chocolate syrup and caramel sauce and serve—if you dare.

"We elves try to stick to the four main food groups: candy, candy canes, candy corn and syrup."
—Buddy

2003

Pastry is put to nefarious work in one of the many scenes that won Christoph Waltz his well-deserved Oscar. Playing Colonel Hans Landa, he uses food as a means of torture when he intimidates Shosanna, a young Jewish theater owner. She is to eat her strudel exactly as he instructs ("attendez la crème"). Murder and war crimes take a backseat when the flaky confection is finally eaten: a satisfying plop as the whipped cream is doled out, an audible crunch emanating from the layers of pastry and butter, and the sounds of our hearts breaking as Hans plunges a cigarette into his dessert.

OSCAR-WORTHY
FOOD PERFORMANCE

No. 9

THE STRUDEL

—— FROM ——

INGLOURIOUS
BASTERDS

2009

BUTTER-POACHED LOBSTER WITH LEMON-BUTTER SAUCE

In *Annie Hall*, Woody Allen and Diane Keaton wrestle these crustacean sea spiders in a kitchen scene that provides comedic relief to their otherwise complicated relationship. But lobsters weren't always so entertaining: they were once considered trash food, served to prison inmates and the poor. Like so many modern delicacies, what was once discarded is now treasured—and expensive! As such, lobster should be prepared simply, joined by modest accompaniments that only serve to accentuate its flavor. Once you've mustered the courage to pick the little beasts up off the floor, that is.

Ingredients

Makes 2 servings

1 pound (4 sticks) unsalted butter

Two 1½- to 2-pound live lobsters

¼ cup white wine vinegar

Finely grated zest of 1 lemon

2 tablespoons finely chopped chives

In a saucepan, melt the butter over medium heat and cook until the foaming subsides, about 2 to 3 minutes. Strain the butter through a fine-mesh sieve lined with several layers of cheesecloth into a bowl and let cool to room temperature, skimming off any impurities that rise to the surface. Set aside.

Prepare the lobsters: Using a large, sharp knife, press the tip down, hard, just behind the eyes of the lobster, then rock the knife downward to split its head in half.

Bring a large pot of salted water to a boil and add the vinegar. Place the lobsters in the boiling water and turn off the heat. Cover the pot and let steep for 3 minutes, then transfer the lobsters to a cutting board. When they're cool enough to handle, remove the meat from the claws and tail and set aside.

Using kitchen shears, cut the shells into 1-inch pieces. In a large skillet, heat the clarified butter and shells at a bare simmer for 20 minutes. In the last 3 minutes of cooking, add the lemon zest. Strain the butter through a fine-mesh sieve and return it to the skillet over medium-low heat. Place the lobster meat in the hot butter and poach, turning frequently, until the internal temperature reaches 145°, about 5 minutes. Remove the skillet from the heat and transfer the lobster and butter to a shallow bowl. Garnish with chives and serve.

"We should have gotten steaks.
They don't have legs, they don't run around."
—Alvy Singer

1977

INSPIRED BY

ANNIE HALL

★ BUTTERBEER ★

In the Harry Potter universe, the Three Broomsticks Inn is synonymous with letting loose and having fun on the weekend. This popular watering hole in the village of Hogsmeade is akin to a favorite dive bar for the wizarding crowd, and the drink of choice for most patrons is butterbeer. Think creamy, frothy and comforting pints of absolute magic. Muggles have recently been privy to an official version that's served at the Orlando amusement park the Wizarding World of Harry Potter. For those of us who can't make the trip to the life-size replica of Diagon Alley, this cold and boozy adaptation—anchored by the cream soda and sweet punch of the butterscotch schnapps—will have to do. Bottoms up!

Ingredients

Makes 4 drinks

2 large egg whites

6 ounces butterscotch schnapps (or butterscotch syrup for a nonalcoholic version)

2 tablespoons simple syrup (1 part sugar shaken with 1 part water until dissolved)

2 teaspoons pure vanilla extract

¼ cup heavy cream

4 cups (32 ounces) cream soda, chilled

In a cocktail shaker, combine the egg whites, butterscotch schnapps, simple syrup, vanilla and cream. Shake vigorously for 20 seconds. Add ½ cup of ice to the shaker and shake again until chilled, about 10 seconds.

Fill 4 chilled mugs about three-quarters full of cream soda. Top each with a quarter of the egg-white mixture and serve.

"Why don't we go and have a butterbeer in the Three Broomsticks, it's a bit cold, isn't it?"

—Hermione Granger

★ CAILLES EN SARCOPHAGE ★

This "quail in sarcophagus" might not be the most appetizingly named dish, but it is one of the most mouthwatering entrées to appear on screen in this classic foodie epic. Like an old-world deconstructed chicken potpie, the dish featured in the film is an exercise in extravagance thanks to its foie gras, black truffle, game birds and buttery pastry. Since we can't all win the lottery to finance dinner tonight, here's a more economical—but nevertheless resplendent—take on Babette's poultry feast.

Ingredients

Makes 2 servings

All-purpose flour, for dusting

One 8-ounce sheet frozen puff pastry, thawed

2 large eggs

4 tablespoons vegetable oil

½ small onion, finely chopped

4 ounces fresh pork sausage, casings removed

4 ounces chicken livers, chopped

1 tablespoon chopped sage

2 tablespoons whole milk

¼ cup dry breadcrumbs

2 tablespoons chopped parsley

One Cornish game hen (about 1 pound)

Kosher salt and freshly ground black pepper

½ cup sherry

½ cup chicken stock

1 tablespoon chopped rosemary

1 tablespoon cold unsalted butter

1 tablespoon truffle oil

4 figs, quartered

Preheat the oven to 425°. Dust a surface with flour and gently roll out the thawed puff pastry. Using a 6-inch bowl as a template, use a paring knife to cut out two rounds of pasty, then place them on a parchment paper–lined baking sheet. Using a 4-inch round pastry cutter (or drinking glass and paring knife), carefully cut a ring in the center of the pastry rounds, making sure to pierce the surface of the pastry but not to cut all the way through. Place the pastry on a baking sheet.

In a small bowl, beat 1 of the eggs. Brush the pastries liberally with the egg and bake for 10 minutes, or until puffed. Reduce the heat to 375° and bake for 5 to 10 minutes longer, or until golden brown. Transfer the baking sheet to a wire rack and let the puff pastries cool completely. Remove the pre-cut center of the pastries to create two "bowls" and two "lids."

In a nonstick skillet, heat 1 tablespoon of the vegetable oil over medium-high heat until shimmering. Add the onion, lower the heat to medium and cook, stirring occasionally, until soft and translucent, about 10 minutes. Add the sausage, breaking it up into small pieces with a wooden spoon, and cook for 3 minutes. Add the chicken livers and cook until the livers and sausage are browned but still pink in the center, about 5 minutes longer. Stir in the sage. Remove the skillet from the heat and let the mixture cool completely. In a large bowl, combine the milk, breadcrumbs, the remaining egg and parsley until well mixed. Add the sausage-liver mixture and mix until the stuffing is combined.

Increase the oven to 400°. Rub the hen all over with 1 tablespoon of vegetable oil and season liberally with salt and pepper. Stuff the cavity with the stuffing and tie the legs together with butcher's twine. In a large skillet, heat the remaining 2 tablespoons of vegetable oil over medium-high heat until nearly smoking. Place the hen, breast side down, in the pan. Sear until the breast is golden brown, then turn the hen over and place the skillet in the oven. Roast for 45 to 55 minutes, or until an instant-read thermometer inserted into the center of the stuffing registers 160°. Transfer the hen to a cutting board and let rest. Place the skillet over medium heat. When the drippings in the pan begin to sizzle, add the sherry and chicken stock, scraping up any browned bits with a wooden spoon. Add the rosemary, bring the liquid to a simmer and reduce by two-thirds. Whisk in the butter and cook at a bare simmer until the sauce is thick enough to coat the back of a spoon.

Place the puff pastry bowls on 2 plates. Carve the hen and place a leg and some of the stuffing in each pastry bowl. Slice the breasts and arrange alongside the bowls. Spoon the sauce around the outside of the plate and over the hens, then lightly drizzle with truffle oil. Scatter the figs around the plates and serve the dish with the pastry "lids" leaning against the bowls.

1987

Gene Wilder's waltz through his fantastical garden of confections isn't just one of the defining moments of your childhood—it's one of the earliest examples of high-fructose hedonism in film. Chocolate greedily lapped up by the fistful, mouthfuls of mammoth gummy bears, mushrooms filled with whipped cream, all permanently emblazoned on your sweet-toothed childhood memories. Can't you remember exactly how the little flower cup, delicately sipped empty of its candy nectar, sounds when it's eaten with a crunch?

THE
"EVERYTHING
EATABLE" ROOM

FROM

WILLY WONKA &
THE CHOCOLATE
FACTORY

1971

CHEDDAR GRITS WITH EGGS AND BACON

Joe Pesci's Cousin Vinny experiences a real culture shock during his time in Alabama—highlighted perfectly by his surprise at a grits and bacon breakfast. He's given an education on how real Southerners cook their grits—something that will eventually turn out to be a vital piece of courtroom information. While a half-pound scoop of lard certainly isn't necessary to recreate this Southern favorite, the addition of some cheese and scallions makes it something everyone can enjoy.

Ingredients

Makes 4 servings

4 cups water

1 teaspoon kosher salt

2 tablespoons unsalted butter

1 cup old-fashioned (not instant) white grits

½ cup whole milk

8 ounces cheddar cheese, grated

1 pound sliced bacon

2 tablespoons lard

4 eggs

2 scallions, greens thinly sliced

Preheat the oven to 350°.

In a medium saucepan, bring the water and salt to a boil. Add 1 tablespoon of the butter and the grits and lower the heat to medium low. Cook, stirring occasionally, until the grits have absorbed the water and are softened, around 15 minutes. Add the milk and cook for 5 minutes longer, then remove the pan from the heat and stir in the cheddar until it's melted. Cover and keep warm until ready to serve.

Line a rimmed baking sheet with aluminum foil and place a wire rack on top. Arrange the bacon on the rack and bake until crisp, about 20 minutes.

In a large nonstick skillet, melt the lard over medium heat until shimmering. Crack the eggs, one at a time, into the pan. Cook until the whites are half-set, about 2 minutes. Cover the pan and cook until the whites are set and yolks are still runny, 1 to 2 minutes longer.

Divide the grits among plates, top with the remaining tablespoon of butter and sprinkle with the scallion greens. Divide the eggs and bacon among the plates and serve.

Cook: "You never heard of grits?"

Vinny: "Sure I heard of grits. I just actually never seen a grit before."

1992

INSPIRED BY

MY COUSIN VINNY

★ CHEESE SOUFFLÉ ★

Soufflé used as a metaphor for love, and not a single filling sprinkled in for good measure? It must have been the 1950s. What was supposed to be an ethereal cloud of cheese and egg falls flat for Audrey Hepburn in *Sabrina*, as she is unhappily in love. Many superstitions surround the rise and fall of the infamously finicky soufflé, so we advise falling thoroughly and happily in love before attempting to bake one.

Ingredients

Makes 4 servings

3 tablespoons unsalted butter, softened

¼ cup finely grated Parmesan cheese

1 cup whole milk

¼ cup all-purpose flour

1 teaspoon kosher salt

½ teaspoon freshly grated nutmeg

5 large eggs, whites and yolks separated

1½ teaspoons Dijon mustard

½ teaspoon cayenne pepper

6 ounces shredded Gruyère cheese

Preheat the oven to 375° and place a rack in the center position.

Brush a 6-cup soufflé dish with 1½ tablespoons of butter. Sprinkle the dish with the Parmesan and rotate until it's well coated. Dump out the excess cheese.

In a large saucepan, heat the milk over medium-low heat until it reaches 190° on an instant-read thermometer. In a separate large saucepan, melt the remaining 1½ tablespoons of butter until the foaming subsides. Add the flour and cook, whisking constantly, until lightly browned and toasty-smelling, about 2 minutes. Add the warm milk and whisk until thickened and free of clumps. Remove the pan from the heat and whisk in the salt and nutmeg. Add the egg yolks, one at a time, whisking until combined. Set the mixture aside and let cool to room temperature. Add the mustard, cayenne and Gruyère and stir until combined.

In the bowl of a stand mixer fitted with a whisk, beat the egg whites until stiff peaks form. Scoop half of the egg whites into the milk-and-egg-yolk mixture and gently fold until combined. Add the remaining egg whites and fold until just combined. Pour the mixture into the prepared soufflé dish, filling it up to about ½ inch from the top (you might have a little leftover batter).

Place the dish in the center of the oven and bake, keeping the oven door closed for the first 20 minutes, until the soufflé has risen and turns golden brown on top but still jiggles slightly when touched, 25 to 30 minutes total. Carefully remove from the oven and serve hot.

"A woman happily in love, she burns the soufflé. A woman unhappily in love, she forgets to turn on the oven."
—Baron St. Fontanel

1954

INSPIRED BY

SABRINA

CHICKEN WITH MOLE AND SAFFRON RICE

In a scene that scared off a generation of home cooks from using a pressure cooker, Holly Golightly's (attempted) romantic dinner comes to an abrupt end when her saffron rice quite literally explodes. To ensure you don't end up coating your entire kitchen in rice, we've adapted this classic pressure-cooker recipe to a safer stovetop version. Also, try to find a guy who's a bit more receptive to chicken and sauce than Paul Varjak. What kind of guy doesn't like chicken and sauce? And why did Audrey Hepburn get all the great food scenes?

Ingredients

Makes 2 servings

- 2 pinches saffron threads
- 1 tablespoon vegetable oil
- 4 boneless, skinless chicken thighs
- Kosher salt
- 2 onions, finely chopped
- 4 garlic cloves, crushed
- 1½ cups chicken stock
- Juice and zest from 1 medium orange
- 1 teaspoon ground cumin
- 2 ounces dried cascabel chiles, seeded and cut into 1-inch pieces
- ½ ounce dried pasilla chiles, seeded and cut into 1-inch pieces
- 1 teaspoon dried oregano
- ¼ teaspoon cinnamon
- ¼ teaspoon ground cloves
- ½ teaspoon allspice
- ¼ cup raisins
- ¼ cup peanuts
- 2 ounces dark chocolate, chopped
- 2 tablespoons unsalted butter
- 3½ cups chicken stock or water, plus more if needed
- 2 cups basmati rice
- 3 tablespoons chopped cilantro, for garnish

Place ½ cup of hot water in a small bowl. Add the saffron threads and let soak for 30 minutes.

In a Dutch oven, heat the oil over medium-high heat until shimmering. Season the chicken with salt and sear on both sides until lightly browned. Remove the chicken from the pan, place on a plate and set aside. Add half the onions and cook, stirring, until softened, about 5 minutes. Add the garlic and cook, stirring, until fragrant, about 1 minute. Deglaze the pan with the 1½ cups of chicken stock, scraping up the browned bits from the bottom of the pan with a wooden spoon. Add the orange juice, orange zest, cumin, cascabel and pasilla chiles, oregano, cinnamon, cloves, allspice, raisins, peanuts and a generous pinch of salt. Stir well to combine and return the chicken to the pan. Cover the pan with the lid slightly ajar and simmer until the chicken is cooked through and the dried chiles have softened, about 20 minutes.

Remove the chicken from the pan and set aside; pour the contents of the pan into a blender. Blend at high speed until completely smooth (if the sauce is too thick, add a splash of water or stock). Wipe out the pan and add the puréed sauce. Add the chocolate and stir over medium-low heat until the chocolate is melted and the sauce is smooth. Place the chicken in the sauce, cover and keep warm until ready to serve.

In a separate saucepan, melt the butter over medium-low heat until the foaming subsides. Add the remaining onion and cook, stirring, until translucent, 3 to 5 minutes. Add the saffron-infused water, the 3½ cups of stock (or water) and 1 teaspoon of salt and bring to a boil. Add the rice, cover and simmer until the rice has absorbed the liquid, 16 to 18 minutes. Turn off the heat and let the rice steam, covered, for 5 minutes. Remove the lid and fluff with a fork. Season to taste with salt.

Divide the rice, chicken and sauce between 2 plates, garnish with cilantro and serve.

"Look, I'm not much for chicken with sauce anyway!"
—Paul Varjak

1961

★ CHOCOLATE TRUFFLES ★

Johnny Depp is at his best when he throws on an accent, lets his hair grow long and unbuttons 90 percent of his shirt—all feats he accomplishes in this film (and many, many others, to be honest) while sensually munching on chocolate. But chocolate—not Mr. Depp's Roux—is the central character in this classic, which juxtaposes the mentality of a small town with the free-spirited rebellion of the main character, played by Juliette Binoche. It's quite literally Vianne's chocolate creations that help the townspeople soften their prudish attitudes and ignite their long-forgotten passions. To celebrate all our guilty pleasures, this simple, adaptable recipe combines chocolate ganache and a flavor or liqueur of your choice. When you combine truffles with home screening of *Chocolat* on a rainy evening, they're essentially edible pheromones.

Ingredients

Makes 16 truffles

8 ounces 70% or higher dark chocolate, chopped

5 tablespoons heavy cream

1 tablespoon unsalted butter

½ cup unsweetened cocoa powder

Optional flavorings:

2 tablespoons whiskey

1 teaspoon pure vanilla extract

5 mint leaves, very finely chopped

1 tablespoon amaretto

1 tablespoon Grand Marnier

2 teaspoons rosewater

Place a bowl over a saucepan of simmering water (or prepare a double boiler). Add the chocolate, cream and butter. Stir constantly until the chocolate has melted completely and the mixture has thickened. Remove the pan from the heat, stir in the flavoring of your choice, if desired, and let cool at room temperature until the chocolate is firm, about 2 hours.

Place the cocoa powder in a wide, shallow bowl. Using a melon baller, scrape the ganache into ¾-inch balls. Moisten your hands with water and roll a chocolate ball gently between your palms until it's round and smooth. Place the ball in the cocoa powder and roll until coated, then transfer to wax paper. Repeat with the remaining chocolate. The truffles will keep for up to 1 week stored in an airtight container in the refrigerator.

"These are for your husband…to awaken the passions."

—Vianne Rocher

2000

One of the most satisfying payoffs ever seen on film, the sight of our stoner heroes finally tearing into a mountain of burgers with reckless abandon is pure culinary catharsis. Sure, the film might be a 90-minute commercial for White Castle, and sure, White Castle might punch holes in their burgers, but in that moment, we're all stoned out of our minds, and we're all finally getting what we crave.

THE BURGERS

—— FROM ——

HAROLD & KUMAR GO
TO WHITE CASTLE

2004

★ CONFIT BYALDI ★

Remy, the preternaturally talented young rat-chef in *Ratatouille*, is propelled to the title of "the finest chef in France" thanks to this vegetable dish he serves to a food critic. The French will be quick to correct you if you were to call Remy's signature dish ratatouille, and that's because the dish in the movie is actually an interpretation concocted by none other than the esteemed chef Thomas Keller, who served as the movie's food consultant. Attractive and delicious, it's sure to soften even the most cold-hearted antagonist into cracking a smile and greedily chowing down.

Ingredients

Makes 4 servings

6 large Roma tomatoes

2 red bell peppers

½ cup vegetable stock

½ cup water

2 tablespoons fresh rosemary

1 teaspoon thyme leaves

1 garlic clove

½ small onion

3 tablespoons olive oil

Kosher salt and freshly ground black pepper

2 medium green squash

2 medium yellow squash

2 medium Japanese eggplants

Coarsely chopped parsley

Bring a medium saucepan of water to a boil. Prepare an ice bath. Cut a small X into the bottom of 4 of the tomatoes. Blanch the tomatoes for 45 seconds. Using a slotted spoon, transfer the tomatoes to the ice bath and let cool completely, then drain. Using a paring knife, peel and discard the tomato skins and set the tomatoes aside.

Turn a stovetop gas burner to high and place the bell peppers on the grate over the flame. (Alternatively, place the peppers on a rimmed baking sheet and broil on high heat.) Blacken the pepper on all sides. Remove the peppers from the flame (or oven), place in a bowl and cover with plastic wrap. Let the peppers steam for 5 minutes, then peel them and discard the stems and seeds. Place the peppers in a high-powered blender or food processor, along with the remaining 2 tomatoes, stock, water, 1 tablespoon of the rosemary, the thyme, garlic, onion, 1 tablespoon of the oil and a pinch of salt. Blend at high speed until completely smooth.

Preheat the oven to 225°. Using a very sharp knife, cut the blanched tomatoes into ⅛-inch slices. Using a mandoline, slice all of the squash and the eggplants into ⅛-inch-thick rounds. Add a thin layer of the roasted pepper mixture to a shallow casserole and spread it across the bottom evenly. Starting with a slice of eggplant, followed by a slice of tomato, a slice of yellow squash and a slice of green squash, begin layering the sliced vegetables around the outer edge of the casserole like shingles, leaving about ¼ inch of overlap between slices. Once the outer ring is complete, create another layer inside that one and continue until the casserole is filled with vegetables. Finely chop the remaining tablespoon of rosemary and sprinkle on top. Drizzle with 1 tablespoon of the oil and season with salt and pepper. Cut a piece of parchment paper the size of the casserole and place it on top of the vegetables. Roast for about 1 hour and 30 minutes; remove the parchment after about 1 hour and 10 minutes of cooking. The vegetables should be completely softened but still hold their shape.

Place a ring mold in the center of a large plate and fill it with vegetables stacked vertically. Place a layer of vegetables staggered horizontally over the top, then slowly remove the ring mold. Combine 1 tablespoon of the red pepper sauce from the bottom of the casserole with the remaining tablespoon of oil, then drizzle it in a circle around the outside of the vegetable stack. Garnish with the parsley and serve.

2007

INSPIRED BY

RATATOUILLE

★ COURTESAN AU CHOCOLAT ★

If Wes Anderson's aesthetic manifested itself as a food, it would be Courtesan au Chocolate, a pastry tower of exquisite beauty and charm. Featured in *The Grand Budapest Hotel*, they are a symbol of love for one character, a means of escape for another. Courtesan au Chocolat is a delicious albeit fussy little dessert that will certainly wow your dinner guests. Here's the recipe you've been dying to try since you saw it on the big screen.

Ingredients

Makes 12 servings

For the pâte à choux:

1 cup all-purpose flour

Kosher salt

Granulated sugar

1 cup water

8 tablespoons (1 stick) unsalted butter

4 large eggs

For the crème pâtissière:

¼ cup granulated sugar

1 tablespoon all-purpose flour

1½ teaspoon cornstarch

3 large egg yolks

2 cups whole milk

8 ounces dark chocolate, chopped

For the icing:

3 cups confectioners' sugar

1 cup plus 1 tablespoon whole milk, plus more as needed

Purple, green, pink and blue food colorings

4 tablespoons (½ stick) unsalted butter

For assembly:

4 ounces white chocolate

Yellow food coloring

12 raw cacao beans

Make the pâte à choux: Preheat the oven to 400°. In a bowl, whisk together 1 cup of flour, a pinch of salt and a pinch of granulated sugar and set aside. In a saucepan over medium heat, combine the water and butter, stirring until the butter has melted. Add the flour mixture and, using a wooden spoon, stir over medium-low heat until the dough pulls away from the side of the pan and forms a ball. Remove from the heat and let cool for 1 minute before adding the eggs; stir until well mixed. (It might seem as though the dough is not coming together at first; keep stirring until it does.) Fill a pastry bag with the choux dough and line two baking sheets with parchment paper or silicone baking mats. Pipe 12 each of ½-inch, 1-inch and 1½-inch rounds of dough onto the prepared baking sheets. Bake until the dough has risen and is golden brown, 15 to 20 minutes for the smaller rounds and 20 to 25 minutes for the larger ones. Transfer them to a wire rack and let cool completely.

Make the crème pâtissière: In a large bowl, whisk together the sugar, flour, cornstarch and egg yolks. In a saucepan, warm the milk over medium-low heat until steaming. Add the chocolate and whisk until completely melted (do not let boil). Whisking constantly, pour half of the chocolate mixture into the flour-and-egg mixture, beating until fully incorporated. Return this mixture to the remaining milk-and-chocolate mixture in the saucepan and stir over low heat until thickened to a pudding-like consistency. Refrigerate until cooled completely.

Make the icings: Place 1 cup of the confectioners' sugar in a bowl and slowly add 1 cup of milk, whisking constantly, until the mixture is a thin glaze. Divide the icing into 3 bowls and add the purple, green and pink food colorings (one for each bowl), stirring until the desired color is reached. In a bowl, combine the remaining 2 cups of confectioners' sugar, the remaining 4 tablespoons of butter and 1 tablespoon of milk. With an electric hand mixer running, slowly beat in more milk as necessary until a thick frosting forms. Place in a bowl and add the blue food coloring.

Assemble the Courtesan au Chocolat: Using a paring knife, make a small hole in the bottom of each choux ball. Pipe each choux full of crème pâtissière. Dip the top the top of the choux in the colored icings: purple for the largest, green for medium and pink for the smallest. Place on a wire rack to set. In a double boiler, melt the white chocolate completely and let sit until it's cool enough to touch. Add yellow food coloring and transfer to a pastry bag fitted with a small tip. Pipe a filigree of white chocolate on each choux ball. Pipe a dollop of blue icing on the center of a large choux ball and top with a medium choux, then top with another dollop of blue icing and a small choux. Add another dot of blue icing to the top of the small choux and place a cacao bean on top of the stack. Repeat with the remaining choux and serve.

2014

★ DINNER ROLLS ★

Charlie Chaplin's legend lies in the physicality of his comedy, but few of his elaborate stunts are more celebrated than a simple tabletop performance with dinner rolls impaled on the tines of forks to resemble tiny dancing feet. When *The Gold Rush* premiered in 1925, audiences were said to be so feverishly amused by the bread routine that some insisted projectionists rewind the scene and play it again, begging the question: Was Charlie Chaplin the first person to play with his food on the big screen? Times have certainly changed, but the scene is cemented in food-film history—and incidentally, the rolls look crusty and delicious.

Ingredients

Makes 12 rolls

1 cup warm water plus ½ cup room-temperature water

16 ounces all-purpose flour

½ teaspoon instant yeast

2 teaspoons salt

Vegetable oil, for the work surface

1 large egg white, beaten

In the bowl of a stand mixer, combine the room-temperature water, 4½ ounces of the flour and the yeast. Whisk well until combined, then cover with plastic wrap and let sit at room temperature for at least 12 hours.

Place the bowl in the stand mixer and fit with the paddle attachment. Add the warm water, the remaining 11½ ounces of flour and the salt and knead for 3 to 5 minutes, until a smooth, tacky (but not sticky) dough forms. Transfer the dough to a lightly oiled large bowl, cover with a clean towel and let rise for 2 hours and 30 minutes.

Turn the dough out onto a lightly oiled surface and knead until smooth and supple. Divide the dough into 12 equal pieces. Roll each piece into a "torpedo" by creating a small rectangle of dough, folding in the corners and kneading until a cylinder with pointed ends forms. Place the rolls, seam side down, on a parchment paper–lined baking sheet, cover with a clean, slightly moist kitchen towel and let rise in a warm place until the rolls have nearly doubled in size, about 1 hour and 30 minutes.

Preheat the oven to 425°. Using a razor blade or very sharp knife, make a lengthwise slash about ¼ inch deep across the top of each roll. Just before placing the rolls in the oven, mist them with water from a spray bottle. Bake the rolls for 15 minutes, then quickly brush the tops with the egg white. Continue baking until the rolls are deep golden brown, about 5 to 15 minutes longer. Transfer the baking sheet to a wire rack and let the rolls cool for at least an hour before serving.

1925

INSPIRED BY

THE GOLD RUSH

DOUBLE-DECKER NEW YORK–STYLE PIZZA

When you're strutting to the beat of the Bee Gees in Angels Flight pants and platform shoes down a 1977 New York sidewalk with a can of paint and era-appropriate lechery, you don't have time to eat your pizza one slice at a time. Tony Manero stops at a Brooklyn institution, Lenny's, for his two slices—stacked atop one another like the Travolta-disco combo that made this movie an international success. This pizza-making method, while employing some modern techniques, results in the classic thin, chewy New York crust that's best eaten two at a time.

Ingredients

Makes two 14-inch pizzas

16 ounces bread flour, plus more for dusting

1 tablespoon plus ½ teaspoon sugar

3 teaspoons kosher salt

½ teaspoon instant yeast

1¼ cups ice water, plus more as necessary

1 tablespoon vegetable oil, plus more for kneading

One 28-ounce can whole peeled tomatoes

2 medium garlic cloves, minced

1 teaspoon dried oregano

½ teaspoon red pepper flakes

½ teaspoon dried basil

¼ cup semolina flour

8 ounces whole-milk mozzarella, shredded

"Gimme two."
—Tony Manero

In a food processor, pulse together the flour, 1 tablespoon of the sugar, 2 teaspoons of the salt and the yeast until well combined. Combine the ice water and oil, then, with the machine running, slowly drizzle through the feed tube until a sticky ball of dough forms. Transfer to an oiled surface and knead until smooth, about 2 minutes. Transfer to an oiled bowl, cover with plastic wrap and refrigerate overnight.

Remove the dough from the refrigerator and divide into two pieces. Wrap each piece of dough in plastic wrap and let rest at room temperature for 1 hour. While the dough rests, prepare the sauce. In a food processor, combine the tomatoes, garlic, oregano, red pepper flakes, basil and the remaining teaspoon of salt. Taste the sauce and, if needed, add the remaining ½ teaspoon of sugar. Process until smooth, then transfer to a saucepan. Bring to a gentle simmer over medium-low heat, then cover and cook for 30 minutes.

Place a pizza stone in the oven and preheat to 550° (or its highest setting) for 1 hour.

Dust a pizza peel or cookie sheet with half of the semolina flour. Generously flour a work surface and place one of the pieces of dough on top. Using your fingertips and pressing gently, push the dough out to form a disc, leaving the edge slightly thicker. Once the dough is about 8 inches wide, pick it up and drape it over your knuckles, letting gravity stretch out the dough. Pass the dough hand over hand, until it's stretched into about a 14-inch round. Place the dough on the pizza peel and reshape into a circle, if needed, leaving the edge slightly thicker. Ladle about ½ cup of sauce onto the dough and spread around until evenly coated. Scatter half of the mozzarella over the top, making sure not to get any sauce or cheese on the raised edge of the dough. Slide the pizza onto the preheated pizza stone and bake until the crust is well browned and the cheese is bubbly and browned in spots, about 12 minutes. Use the pizza peel to remove the pie and transfer it to a large cutting board or pizza pan. Repeat with the remaining ingredients to make a second pie, then place the second pizza, cheese side up, over the first. Using a pizza cutter or large knife, cut the double-stacked pizzas into slices and serve.

1977

A standout scene for its demonstration of pure culinary prowess, the feast prepared during the opening credits of *Eat Drink Man Woman* is a seafood lover's fever dream. The cooking sounds alone earn it a place on this list: the wet smacks of a sharp blade chopping peppers, the pitter patter of bubbles emanating from a simmering pot of seafood, the thunderous cackle of hot oil hitting a piece of expertly butchered fish. It's not unlike the great documentary *Jiro Dreams of Sushi*, in which the viewer sees the unwavering stare and steady hand of a master craftsman at work, at once as motivating as it is appetizing.

THE OPENING
DINNER SCENE

——— FROM ———

EAT DRINK
MAN WOMAN

1994

EGGS IN A NEST WITH RED PEPPER SAUCE

Eggs in a nest is a surprisingly pervasive dish in cinema and television, making appearances in *Moonstruck*, *Friends*, *V for Vendetta*, and its debut in *Mary Jane's Pa* in 1935. It's a favorite comfort food for a wide variety of characters. Even more than movie credits, this dish has an endless list of names: "toad in the hole," "eggs in a basket," "gashouse eggs" and the ever-appetizing "spit in the ocean." No matter what you call it, Olympia Dukakis's character in *Moonstruck* uses roasted red peppers as a lively addition to this beloved breakfast treat.

Ingredients   *Makes 2 servings*

Five 1-inch slices of Italian bread

4 ounces jarred roasted red peppers

½ garlic clove

½ cup vegetable or chicken stock

½ small onion

1 teaspoon thyme leaves

1 teaspoon kosher salt

1 tablespoon olive oil

3 tablespoons unsalted butter

4 large eggs

Salt and freshly ground black pepper

1 tablespoon thinly sliced scallion greens

In a high-powered blender, combine 1 slice of bread (torn into pieces), the red peppers, garlic, stock, onion, thyme and salt. Blend at high speed for 6 minutes, adding the oil to blend smoothly, or until piping hot (the blender will cook the vegetables); set aside.

Cut or tear 3-inch holes in the center of each of the remaining 4 slices of bread. In a large nonstick skillet, melt the butter over medium heat until the foaming subsides. Add the bread and toast until the bottom is golden brown, 2 to 3 minutes. Crack the eggs into the center of each slice of bread and continue cooking until the egg whites are half-set. Flip the bread and continue cooking until the egg whites are completely set and the yolk is still runny.

Spoon some of the red pepper sauce onto 2 plates. Place 2 eggs in a nest on each plate, season with salt and pepper, garnish with the scallions and serve.

"They say bread is life. And I bake bread, bread, bread. And I sweat and shovel this stinkin' dough in and out of this hot hole in the wall, and I should be so happy! Huh, sweetie?"
—Ronny Cammareri

1987

ESCARGOTS IN GARLIC BUTTER

In her role as streetwalker Vivian Ward, Julia Roberts not only won a Golden Globe, but also the adoration of the entire nation. *Pretty Woman* remains one of the most successful romantic comedies of all time, which is stunning when you consider that it's essentially a "modern" (read: 1990s) retelling of Pygmalion, one of the most intolerable plays you were forced to read in high school. The cultural divide in this film is illustrated, as it often is, with food. Vivian can't quite wrap her head (or utensils) around some of the froufrou courses served at a fancy dinner she attends with Edward. You, on the other hand, can turn snails into a daring starter for your next dinner party.

Ingredients

Makes 4 servings

½ pound (2 sticks) European-style butter, softened

1 tablespoon kosher salt

1 teaspoon freshly ground black pepper

1 shallot, finely chopped

6 garlic cloves, finely chopped

½ cup finely chopped parsley

¼ cup sherry

1 cup rock salt

24 canned snails

24 snail shells (optional)

12 slices country bread, toasted

Preheat the oven to 425°. In the bowl of a stand mixer fitted with a paddle, combine the butter, kosher salt, pepper, shallot, garlic, half of the parsley and the sherry. Beat at medium speed until well combined.

Fill a small baking dish (large enough to fit all the snails) with enough rock salt to make a ½-inch layer covering the bottom of the dish. Tuck the snails into the shells. Using a small spoon, stuff the shells with the butter mixture. Place the stuffed shells, open side up, on the salt, pressing down slightly to stabilize them. Bake until the butter is bubbling and the snails are very hot, 15 to 20 minutes.

Meanwhile, gently melt the remaining herb butter in a saucepan over low heat. Garnish the escargots with the remaining parsley. Serve with toasted bread and melted herb butter for dipping.

"Slippery little suckers."
—*Vivian Ward*

1990

★ FISH TACOS ★

The comedic bromance *I Love You, Man* contains a surprisingly serious foodie scene—where Sydney (Jason Segel) forces Peter (Paul Rudd) to cancel dinner plans with his fiancé for "the best fish tacos in the world" served at a famous Venice Beach canteen. Grilled mahimahi with a selection of taco accoutrements ("taco-trements"), piled high on fluffy house-made tortillas, is the order of the day. Regardless of whether you choose to make each component from scratch, or substitute any of them with store-bought versions, you'll find that your taco game, along with your appreciation for your best male friend, has changed forever.

Ingredients   *Makes 4 servings*

For the refried beans:

1 tablespoon vegetable oil

¼ cup chopped Spanish onion

2 garlic cloves, finely chopped

8 ounces dry black beans, soaked overnight

2 tablespoons lard, chilled

For the fish:

Juice of one lime

2 teaspoons kosher salt

1 teaspoon freshly ground pepper

1 teaspoon cumin

¼ cup chopped Spanish onion

1 garlic clove, finely chopped

1 pound fresh mahimahi, halibut, or other white fish in one piece

1 tablespoon of vegetable oil

For the tortillas:

9 ounces (about 2 cups) all-purpose flour, plus more for dusting

4 teaspoons baking powder

1 teaspoon kosher salt

3 tablespoons lard, chilled

½ cup warm water

For the pico de gallo:

4 medium Roma tomatoes, seeded and chopped

½ cup chopped Spanish onion

2 tablespoons chopped cilantro

1 jalapeño, seeded and finely chopped

Juice of one lime

Kosher salt

Make the refried beans: Heat the vegetable oil in a skillet over medium-high heat until shimmering. Add the onion and cook, stirring, until translucent, about 5 minutes. Add the garlic and cook until fragrant, about 1 minute, before adding the soaked beans. Add just enough water to cover the beans and simmer until the beans are tender, about 1 hour and 30 minutes.

Heat the lard in a medium skillet over medium heat. Using a slotted spoon, transfer the cooked beans to the skillet, reserving some of the cooking liquid. Cook the beans, stirring and mashing with a wooden spoon until most of the beans are broken down and the mixture is slightly chunky. Keep warm.

Make the fish: Make a marinade by combining the lime juice, salt, pepper, cumin, onions, and garlic in a resealable bag. Add the fish, close the bag, and gently massage to distribute the marinade. Refrigerate for 30 to 60 minutes.

When you're ready to make the fish, preheat the oven to 400°.

In a large ovenproof skillet, heat the vegetable oil over medium-high heat until barely smoking. Add the fish skin side up and sear until browned on the bottom and the fish releases from the pan. Turn the fish over and transfer the skillet to the oven. Roast until the fish is cooked through (an instant-read thermometer inserted into the thicket part of the fish should register 135°), about 10 to 15 minutes. Transfer the fish to a platter, let it rest 5 minutes, and then flake it with a fork or cut into bite-size chunks.

Make the tortillas: In a food processor, combine the flour, baking powder, salt, and lard, pulsing until the mixture resembles wet sand. With the machine running, slowly drizzle the warm water through a feed tube, stopping as soon as a ball of dough forms. Remove the dough and turn it out onto a floured work surface. Knead the dough, adding flour if the dough is too sticky. Continue kneading until the dough is supple and tacky, about 3 minutes. Wrap the dough in plastic and let rest at room temperature for 20 minutes.

Remove the dough from plastic wrap and cover with a damp kitchen towel. Place a dry kitchen towel over a large piece of aluminum foil. Heat a non-stick skillet over a medium-high heat for 2 minutes. Take a golf ball–size piece of dough and toll it out on a well-floured surface into a think round about 8 to 10 inches in diameter.

For the salsa verde:

6 medium tomatillos, peeled, rinsed, and halved

1 tablespoon olive oil

¼ cup chopped Spanish onion

2 tablespoons chopped cilantro

1 jalapeño, seeded and finely chopped

Juice of one lime

Kosher salt

For the guacamole:

4 semi-soft avocados

1 small red onion, finely chopped

Juice of 1 lime

2 tablespoons chopped cilantro

1 teaspoon cumin

1 jalapeño, seeded and finely chopped

1 garlic clove, finely chopped

Kosher salt and freshly ground black pepper

For serving:

¼ cup cotija cheese

Lime wedges, one per taco

Chopped cilantro

Drop the tortilla in the preheated pan and cook until top is bubbling and the underside is lightly browned, about 30 seconds. Flip and cook for 30 seconds longer, then transfer to the clean towel. Repeat with the remaining dough, adjusting the heat as necessary so the tortillas don't burn; they should be soft and pliable, but not blackened. Keep the warm tortillas covered with the kitchen towel and, when the final tortilla is cooked, close the foil over the towel.

Make the pico de gallo: In a medium bowl, combine the Roma tomatoes, onions, cilantro, jalapeño, lime juice, and a pinch of salt. Set aside.

Make the salsa verde: Preheat the broiler to high. In a bowl, toss the tomatillos with olive oil. Arrange tomatillos, cut side down, on a rimmed baking sheet and broil until lightly charred, 3 to 5 minutes. In a food processor, combine the tomatillos, onions, cilantro, jalapeño, and lime juice, and add a pinch of salt. Pulse until a chunky salsa is formed. Set aside.

Make the guacamole: Halve and pit the avocados, then scoop out the flesh. In a large bowl, combine the avocado, red onion, lime juice, cilantro, cumin, jalapeño, and garlic, and mash the mixture with a fork until it reaches the desired consistency. Season to taste with salt and pepper. Cover with plastic wrap, pressing the plastic onto the surface of the guacamole to help prevent it from becoming discolored. Refrigerate until ready to serve.

Assemble the tacos: Spread refried beans over warm tortillas, and sprinkle with cotija cheese. Add the fish pieces next, followed by the salsas and guacamole. Serve with lime wedges and garnished with cilantro.

"No dude, this place has the best fish tacos in the world, literally, ranked. You gotta have one. Or two?"
—Sydney Fife

2009

I LOVE YOU, MAN

FRIED CHICKEN AND CORN ON THE COB

Bob Wiley, a character only Bill Murray could pull off, is the endearingly unstable patient of the especially Richard Dreyfuss-y Dr. Leo Marvin. Their doctor-patient relationship is perfectly encapsulated during a memorable family dinner scene at Dr. Marvin's house, wherein Bob's enthusiastic adulation of fried chicken and corn sends Dr. Marvin over the edge. Follow this simple recipe, which features a few special tricks, to elicit the same chorus of *mmms* from your dinner guests.

Ingredients

Makes 4 servings

3 cups all-purpose flour

2 cups cornflakes, crushed

2 tablespoons paprika

1 tablespoon garlic powder

2 tablespoons kosher salt

1 tablespoon freshly ground black pepper

1 teaspoon cayenne pepper

½ teaspoon baking soda

Juice of 1 lemon

5 large eggs

1 whole chicken, cut into 10 pieces (2 drumsticks, 2 thighs, 2 wings and 4 breast pieces)

3 cups leaf lard

4 ears of corn, shucked

Softened butter, for the corn

In a large bowl, whisk together 2 cups of the flour, the cornflakes, paprika, garlic powder, salt, pepper, cayenne and baking soda. In a separate bowl, whisk together the lemon juice and eggs.

Dry the chicken pieces very well with paper towels. Place the remaining cup of flour in a wide, shallow bowl. Coat a piece of chicken in the flour and knock off the excess. Dip the chicken in the egg mixture, let the excess drip off, then roll in the flour–corn flake mixture until well-coated. Repeat with the remaining chicken.

Meanwhile, heat the lard in a large saucepan or Dutch oven over medium heat until it reaches 350° on a deep-fry thermometer. Preheat the oven to 200° and place a rimmed baking sheet fitted with a wire rack inside. Working in batches, fry the chicken, turning once halfway through cooking, until golden brown and an instant-read thermometer inserted into the thickest part registers 160°, about 5 to 10 minutes. Transfer the fried chicken to the oven to keep warm and repeat with the remaining chicken (let the lard return to 350° between batches).

Bring a large pot of salted water to a boil. Carefully add the corn and boil for 4 minutes. Using tongs, transfer the corn to a platter along with the fried chicken and serve with softened butter.

"Mmm...Fay, this is so scrumptious...
is this hand-shucked?"
—*Bob Wiley*

1991

★ GIANT PANCAKES ★

A book about the foods of film would scarcely be complete without paying tribute to John Candy's gargantuan pancakes made for his nephew's birthday in *Uncle Buck*. Every kid's fantasy materializes with a mountain of pancakes, a river of syrup and a pat of butter the size of a phone book. Most home cooks don't have the gear (or the gumption) to make pancakes that require a snow shovel to flip, so I've adapted Buck's recipe to slightly smaller pizza-size pancakes.

Ingredients

Makes 2 large pancakes (4 servings)

12 tablespoons (1½ stick) unsalted butter

2 cups all-purpose flour

2 tablespoons baking powder

2 tablespoons sugar

4 large eggs

1½ cups whole milk, plus more if needed

Warm maple syrup, for serving

Allow 8 tablespoons of butter to come to room temperature and form it into a large pat about 3 inches square and ½ inch thick. Refrigerate until ready to serve.

In a large bowl, whisk the flour, baking powder and sugar. Whisk in the eggs and 1½ cups of milk until a thick-but-viscous batter is formed, drizzling in more milk if needed.

Preheat the oven to 200° and place an oven-safe plate or platter inside. In a 12-inch nonstick skillet, heat 2 tablespoons of butter over medium-high heat until the foaming subsides. Pour half of the batter into the pan and reduce the heat to medium. Cook until bubbles begin to form on the surface of the pancake, 3 to 5 minutes. Using a large spatula (or two smaller spatulas), flip the pancake over and cook until golden brown on the bottom, 3 to 5 minutes longer. Transfer to the oven to keep warm. Repeat with the remaining butter and batter to make a second pancake.

Stack the pancakes, top with the large pat of butter and serve with warm maple syrup.

"You should see the toast;
I couldn't even get it through the door."
—Buck Russel

1989

A film that blurs the line between documentary and scripted comedy, *The Trip* is an excuse for Rob Brydon and Steve Coogan to goof off while enjoying some of Britain's finest cuisine. Fortunately, the result is as entertaining as it is sumptuous, and The Inn at Whitewell offers our stars some truly stunning dishes. At once brashly contemporary and sweetly familiar, the grilled baby scallops, shellfish broths and herbaceous beverages are the only intermissions from the comedians' legendary impressions of Michael Caine.

THE FOOD SERVED AT
THE INN AT WHITEWALL

—— FROM ——

THE TRIP

2010

★ HAWAIIAN BURGER ★

Vincent Vega and Jules Winnfield are the homicidal pals woven between the careening subplots in Quentin Tarantino's *Pulp Fiction*. Never one to shy away from on-camera cuisine, Tarantino has more than once featured the Big Kahuna Burger in his tales of murderous revenge. But never has a hamburger been eaten with such fierce intimidation as when Jules helps himself to another man's burger and soda right before he fills said man (and his posse) with lead. The scene is memorable for three reasons: It spawned a thousand Internet memes, it takes us to a new level of respect for Marsellus Wallace, and it makes us desperately crave a Hawaiian burger (essentially a cheeseburger with pineapple and teriyaki sauce on top). Although some of us would kill for one, you can skip all that drama and just make your own at home.

Ingredients

Makes 1 burger

2 tablespoons unsalted butter

1 red onion, sliced into rings

Two ½-inch fresh pineapple slices, cored

1 tablespoon vegetable oil

4 ounces ground beef, divided into two balls

2 slices Monterey Jack cheese

1 Hawaiian-style hamburger bun, toasted and buttered

1½ teaspoons ketchup

1½ teaspoons teriyaki sauce

In a large skillet, heat 1 tablespoon of butter over medium heat until foaming. Add the onion and cook slowly over low heat, stirring often, until the onion is caramelized, 30 minutes. Transfer the onion to a bowl and set aside.

Wipe out the skillet and heat the remaining tablespoon of butter over medium heat until sizzling. Add the pineapple slices and cook, turning once, until lightly browned on both sides. Transfer the pineapple to a plate and set aside.

In a large cast-iron skillet, heat the oil over high heat until just beginning to smoke. Place the beef balls several inches apart in the skillet, then use a heavy spatula to smash them down into thin patties (about ¼ to ½ inch thick). Cook until the bottom is well browned and crisp, 1 to 2 minutes, then flip and top with a slice of cheese. Turn off the heat, but leave the patties in the pan while you assemble the burgers (the residual heat will brown the other side).

Dress the bottom half of the bun with ketchup and teriyaki sauce and top with the patties, pineapple and caramelized onion. Top with the other half of the bun and serve.

"Hamburgers!
The cornerstone of any nutritious breakfast."
—Jules Winnfield

1994

★ HAZELNUT GELATO ★

Audrey Hepburn's three appearances in this book are no accident—it only makes sense that films about luxury, love and wanderlust feature food that fits the bill. In *Roman Holiday*, Audrey enjoys some gelato on Rome's Spanish Steps as Gregory Peck encourages her to "take a little time for herself" and "live dangerously" instead of going back to school. And through the power of cinema magic, that cone of gelato, just like Hepburn's short hair and scooter rides, became a symbol of taking a day for yourself and going off on an adventure. Though gelato is said to have been invented in Florence, Rome is as good a place as any to get a top-quality sample of the frozen treat. But since it's easier to make at home than traditional ice cream, you may as well take the day for yourself and whip up some homemade gelato.

Ingredients

Makes 10 servings

6 ounces blanched hazelnuts

2 cups whole milk

1 cup heavy cream

4 large egg yolks

½ cup sugar

2 pounds ice (optional)

½ cup rock salt (optional)

"I'd like to sit at a sidewalk café, look in shop windows, walk in the rain, have fun, maybe some excitement!"
—*Princess Ann*

Preheat the oven to 400°. Scatter the hazelnuts on a rimmed baking sheet and toast until lightly browned. Let cool, then transfer to a food processor. Pulse until finely chopped. Transfer 5 ounces of the hazelnuts to a large saucepan and combine with the milk and cream. Bring to a simmer, remove from the heat and cover. Allow the mixture to steep for 1 hour.

Strain the mixture through a fine-mesh sieve into a bowl and discard the solids. Wipe the saucepan clean and return the liquid to the saucepan.

In a large bowl, use a hand mixer (or large whisk) to beat the egg yolks and sugar together until pale yellow ribbons form when the whisk is lifted out of the mixture, about 2 to 3 minutes. Whisk the eggs into the cream mixture and set the pan over medium-low heat, stirring constantly with a wooden spoon. Once the mixture is thick enough to coat the back of the spoon (or registers 170° on an instant-read thermometer), remove the pan from the heat and transfer the custard to a metal bowl. Refrigerate until completely cooled, at least 3 hours.

Process the gelato in an ice cream maker according to manufacturer's instructions, or use the method below.

In a large metal bowl, combine the ice and rock salt. Press the smaller bowl containing the custard into the middle of the ice until the ice covers all sides of the bowl. Using a hand mixer, beat the custard at medium-high speed for about 10 minutes until it becomes smooth and thick. Place the nested bowls in the freezer for 1 hour, until the custard reaches a pudding-like consistency. Beat again for 5 minutes, until the texture is like soft serve ice cream.

Transfer the frozen custard to a rectangular container, sprinkle with the remaining ounce of toasted hazelnuts and freeze overnight before serving.

1953

★ HORS D'OEUVRES SANDWICH ★

Rodney Dangerfield built a career on his disregard for social convention, and his relationship with hors d'oeuvres in *Back to School* is a shining example. Wasting no time with fussy finger foods, he quickly hollows out a loaf of bread, stuffs it with the dainty snacks and slices it in half proudly. Sometimes when you throw convention out the window and mash everything together, you end up with something great (Thanksgiving leftovers, sushi burritos)—and this sandwich is no exception.

Ingredients

Makes 4 servings

For the meatballs:

1 pound ground beef

1 egg, beaten

¼ cup dry breadcrumbs

½ small yellow onion, chopped

½ cup ketchup

½ cup grape jelly

For the spanakopita:

1 tablespoon unsalted butter

8 ounces baby spinach

2 cloves garlic, minced

¼ pound feta cheese, crumbled

¼ cup fresh dill, chopped

1 sheet frozen puff pastry, thawed

1 egg, beaten

For the deviled eggs:

6 hard-boiled eggs, peeled

2 tablespoons mayonnaise

1 teaspoon white vinegar

½ teaspoon Dijon mustard

¼ teaspoon onion powder

¼ teaspoon celery salt

Pinch of paprika

For the sandwich:

One 1-pound oval-shaped French loaf

Olives (optional)

Cheese cubes (optional)

Crudités (optional)

Parsley, roughly chopped (optional)

Make the meatballs: In a large bowl, mix together the beef, egg, breadcrumbs and onion. Combine the ketchup and grape jelly in a large saucepan and bring to a bare simmer. Form the beef mixture into ¾-inch meatballs and place each one in the ketchup sauce. Simmer the meatballs until cooked through, 15 to 20 minutes.

Make the spanakopita: Preheat the oven to 375°. In a skillet, heat the butter over medium-high heat until foaming. Add the spinach and garlic and cook, stirring frequently, until the spinach is wilted, about 4 minutes. Remove from the heat and let cool slightly. Transfer the cooked spinach to a fine-mesh sieve and, using a spoon, press out as much liquid as possible. Place the spinach in a large bowl, add the feta and dill and stir gently until mixed; set aside.

On a well-floured work surface, roll out the puff pastry to slightly larger than its original size. Cut out 5-inch squares of pastry and place 2 tablespoons of the spinach mixture in one corner of each pastry square, leaving ½ inch of space around the edges. Brush the edges of each pastry with water, then fold the pastry diagonally to create a triangle of stuffed dough. Crimp the edges with a fork and brush the tops with the egg. Transfer the pastry to a baking sheet and bake for 15 to 20 minutes, or until browned and crisp.

Make the deviled eggs: Slice the hard-boiled eggs in half lengthwise and place the yolks in a medium bowl. Add the mayonnaise, vinegar, mustard, onion powder and celery salt. Stir with a fork until well combined. If desired, place the filling in a pastry bag and pipe the mixture into the egg white halves; otherwise, spoon the filling into the eggs. Dust each egg with paprika.

Assemble the sandwich: Cut the bread in half lengthwise and scoop out some of the inside to make room for the hors d'oeuvres. Fill the bottom of the loaf with meatballs, followed by a layer of the spanakopita and a layer of deviled eggs. Add any optional toppings. Top with remaining half of the loaf, cut into 4 large slices and serve.

"I learned this in Europe."
—*Thornton Melon*

1986

★ "I'M SORRY" CARROT CAKE ★

Cake is often the centerpiece of a celebration or commemoration, but rarely is it used as an apology. If, however, you're anything like Annie, a baker with suppressed angst and tons of girl squad problems who's trying to make amends to a guy crush, this is the cake for you. Although carrot cake is traditionally iced with cream cheese frosting, this recipe calls for a cream cheese fondant instead, so the end result can be sculpted into an adorable giant carrot. Even though this cake doesn't guarantee an accepted apology, it will still be delicious.

Ingredients

Makes 1 cake (about 8 servings)

For the cake:

Softened butter, for the pan

3 cups all-purpose flour

½ teaspoon salt

1 teaspoon baking soda

1 teaspoon baking powder

1 tablespoon cinnamon

½ teaspoon ground allspice

½ teaspoon ground ginger

½ teaspoon ground nutmeg

1½ cups vegetable oil

4 large eggs

2 tablespoons pure vanilla extract

1½ cups granulated sugar

1 cup chopped walnuts

1 cup sweetened shredded coconut

2 cups finely grated carrots

1 cup raisins (optional)

For the frosting:

4 tablespoons (½ stick) unsalted butter, softened

12 ounces cream cheese, softened

1 tablespoon pure vanilla extract

2 cups confectioners' sugar

Orange and green fondant, rolled into thin sheets

Make the cake: Preheat the oven to 350°. Cut a sheet of parchment paper to fit the bottom of a 1½-pound loaf pan. Butter the parchment, then butter the pan and line with the parchment paper.

In a medium bowl, whisk together the flour, salt, baking soda, baking powder, cinnamon, allspice, ginger and nutmeg. In the bowl of a stand mixer fitted with a paddle, combine the oil, eggs, vanilla and the granulated sugar. Beat at medium-low speed until creamy. With the mixer running at low speed, slowly add the dry ingredients and mix until smooth. Add the walnuts, coconut, carrots and raisins, if using, and mix until evenly distributed.

Pour the batter into the loaf pan and bake for 45 to 60 minutes, until a tester inserted into the center of the cake comes out clean. Remove the pan from the oven and place on a wire rack. Run a paring knife around the sides of the cake and let cool completely, at least 2 hours.

Make the frosting: In the bowl of a stand mixer fitted with a paddle, combine the butter, 4 ounces of the cream cheese and vanilla. Beat until creamy, then slowly sift in the confectioners' sugar and beat until smooth. Refrigerate until ready to use.

Once the cake has cooled, remove it from the loaf pan. Cut about one-sixth of the cake from one end, slice it in half lengthwise and reserve. Using a bread knife, gradually shave off two sides of the cake until it comes to a point on one end to form the shape of a wide, short carrot. Slice the cake horizontally into two layers. Liberally spread frosting on the bottom half and place the second layer over it. Drape the cake with orange fondant, pressing it down onto the corners. Trim the extra fondant until the cake resembles a carrot. Spread the top of one of the reserved cake pieces with frosting, top with the other reserved cake piece and cut into a trapezoid shape to form the carrot stem. Drape the stem with green fondant, trim and press the stem against the carrot. Using the back of a paring knife, score the cake with decorative ridges.

Transfer the remaining 8 ounces of cream cheese to a pastry bag fitted with a fine tip and write "I'm Sorry" on top of the cake. Slice and serve.

2011

BRIDESMAIDS

This film, one of the greatest achievements in food porn to date, is made all the more impressive by the fact that much of the cooking is done by a rat. Granted, it's a squeaky-clean Pixar rat, but it almost seems like a dare to write a script starring a restaurant's (and diner's) greatest enemy. Even more impressive is a stack of tomatoes and squash as its culinary centerpiece, which convincingly melts the heart of an icy food critic. You've never wanted to eat your vegetables so badly.

CONFIT BYALDI

FROM

RATATOUILLE

2007

NEW YORK–STYLE PASTRAMI ★

When you dine at Manhattan's Katz's Delicatessen, you can see a wooden placard commemorating the spot where Meg Ryan convinced Billy Crystal that he had never, in fact, pleased a woman. You can also order a steaming mountain of impeccably cured, spiced, smoked and steamed beef brisket, otherwise known as pastrami. If you don't happen to be on the Lower East Side, here's how you can enjoy New York–Style Pastrami at home—as long as you have a smoker, some curing salts and are willing to wait a couple of weeks. Serve it on a giant slab of toasted rye with a generous smear of spicy mustard and let your toes curl if you're so moved.

Ingredients

Makes 8 to 10 servings

1 gallon water

10 ounces kosher salt

1 tablespoon saltpeter

1 tablespoon pink curing salt (Prague powder)

½ cup plus 2 tablespoons brown sugar

1 tablespoon mustard seeds

1 tablespoon allspice berries

3 whole cloves

½ teaspoon ground ginger

½ teaspoon red pepper flakes

1 bay leaf, crushed

1 cinnamon stick

4 cloves garlic, smashed

One 4-pound brisket, silver skin trimmed, ½ inch of fat cap left on

3 tablespoons freshly ground black pepper

1 tablespoon ground coriander

2 teaspoons mustard powder

1 tablespoon paprika

1 teaspoon garlic powder

1 teaspoon onion powder

Sliced rye bread, for serving

Spicy mustard, for serving

Pour 1 gallon of water into a large food-safe tub. Add the salt, saltpeter, curing salt, ½ cup of the brown sugar, the mustard seeds, allspice berries, cloves, ginger, red pepper flakes, bay leaf, cinnamon stick and garlic. Stir until the sugar and salts have dissolved. Add the brisket. If the brisket floats, place a bowl filled with brine on top to weigh it down. Cover and refrigerate for at least 5 days and up to 2 weeks, agitating daily to evenly distribute the brine and spices.

Remove the brisket from the brine and discard the contents of the plastic tub. Rinse both with cold water, fill the tub with cold water, place the beef inside and let it soak for 8 hours to desalinate.

Remove the beef from the tub and rinse. In a bowl, combine the black pepper, coriander, mustard powder, paprika, garlic powder, onion powder and the remaining 2 tablespoons of brown sugar. Rub the spice mixture all over the beef, making sure to coat it evenly with a thick crust of the spice mixture. Refrigerate, uncovered, on a rack-lined rimmed baking sheet, for 2 days.

Preheat a smoker to 225° and place the beef inside. Smoke for at least 2 hours, or until an instant-read thermometer inserted into the center of the meat registers 155°.

Place a wire rack inside a large stovetop-safe roasting pan. Fill the pan with about 2 inches of water and place the brisket on top of the rack. Cover the pan tightly with foil, place on top of a burner over medium-low heat until the water begins to simmer. Steam until an instant-read thermometer inserted into the center of the meat registers 200°. Transfer the brisket to a cutting board. Slice and serve with rye bread and spicy mustard.

"I'll have what she's having."

—*Katz's customer*

1989

WHEN HARRY MET SALLY...

★ PASTA AGLIO E OLIO ★

Like food, sometimes movies are greater than the sum of their parts. *Chef*, albeit not cinematically groundbreaking, proved to be a critically lauded gem for foodies. Jon Favreau plays a stubborn chef who decides to carve his own path in the food world by starting a food-truck business. But one of the most memorable dishes from the movie isn't a Cubano he whips up for his customers; it's the Pasta Aglio e Olio he makes for his date, played by Scarlett Johansson, partially to feed and partially to seduce her. A seemingly boring amalgam of a few simple ingredients, this turns out to be an easy-to-make dish perfect for a late night, a date night or any night.

Ingredients

Makes 2 servings

½ cup good-quality olive oil

8 large garlic cloves, very thinly sliced

1 teaspoon red pepper flakes

½ pound dried linguine

½ lemon

Salt and freshly ground black pepper

½ cup finely chopped parsley

In a large skillet, heat the oil over medium heat until barely shimmering. Add the garlic and cook, stirring constantly, until softened and turning golden brown around the edges, taking care not to let the garlic burn. Add the red pepper flakes and remove the skillet from the heat.

Meanwhile, bring a large pot of salted water to a boil. Add the pasta and cook until just shy of al dente. Drain the pasta, reserving ¼ cup of the pasta water. Return the skillet to medium heat and add the drained pasta and a splash of pasta water. Continue cooking the pasta, tossing frequently and adding water as needed, until the pasta is al dente and well coated in a creamy sauce. Squeeze the lemon over the pasta, season to taste with salt and pepper, sprinkle with the parsley and serve.

"I wanna share this with you. I wanna teach you what I learned. I get to touch peoples' lives with what I do, and it keeps me going and I love it, and I think if you give it a shot, you might love it, too."

—Carl Casper

INSPIRED BY

CHEF

2014

PASTA WITH PRISON GRAVY AND MEATBALLS

In addition to heavy cocaine use, surprise garroting and loyalty to their families, movie mobsters often have one more thing in common: They know how to eat well. This is best illustrated in *Goodfellas*, the 1990 Scorsese classic, where a collection of wiseguys whips up a sauce in their prison cell that would put your grandmother's sauce to shame. Brimming with San Marzano tomatoes, laden with meat and lots of onions, and featuring authentic Italian meatballs, Vinnie's Sunday gravy might leave you with an involuntary Brooklyn accent and a bloodlust for shopkeepers who haven't paid their protection dues.

Ingredients

Makes 12 servings

For the gravy:

1 tablespoon vegetable oil

½ pound sweet Italian sausage, casings removed

½ pound spicy Italian sausage, casings removed

½ pound beef shank

½ pound veal neck bones, with meat attached

1 tablespoon olive oil

2 garlic cloves, sliced paper-thin

1 medium onion, finely chopped

1 tablespoon tomato paste

½ cup red wine

Two 28-ounce cans whole peeled San Marzano tomatoes

2 large basil sprigs

1 large carrot, peeled and cut into 3 pieces

1 pound meatballs

1 tablespoon olive oil or butter, for finishing the sauce (optional)

For the meatballs:

2 thick slices Italian bread, torn into small pieces

¼ cup buttermilk, plus more as needed

½ medium onion, finely chopped

3 garlic cloves, finely chopped

2 ounces Parmesan cheese, grated

¼ cup loosely packed fresh parsley leaves, finely chopped

Make the gravy: In a very large nonreactive (stainless steel or enameled cast iron) pot, heat the vegetable oil over medium-high heat until shimmering. Working in batches, brown the sausages, beef and veal until well browned and a brown crust forms on the bottom of the pot. Transfer the meat to a platter and reserve. Heat the olive oil in the same pot over medium heat until shimmering. Add the garlic and cook until soft, about 30 seconds. Add the onion and tomato paste and cook until the onion is translucent, about 4 minutes. Add the wine and stir, making sure to scrape up all the browned bits on the bottom of the pot. Pour the tomatoes into a bowl and crush them with your hands, then add them to the pot. Return the meat and any accumulated juices to the pot. Add the basil and carrot and bring to a gentle simmer.

Let the sauce simmer on low heat for about 4 hours total, stirring and scraping the bottom occasionally with a wooden spoon (don't let anything stick to the pot; it will scorch and ruin your sauce). During the final hour of cooking, add the meatballs to the sauce.

Using tongs, fish out and discard the carrots and bones. If there is any remaining meat on the bones, remove it and put it back in the sauce. If desired, stir in a tablespoon of olive oil or butter to make a richer sauce.

The sauce freezes and reheats exceptionally well for up to 2 months.

Make the meatballs: In a large bowl, combine the bread with the buttermilk, tossing to coat. Let the mixture stand, tossing occasionally, until the bread is completely moist, about 10 minutes. Squeeze the bread between your fingers or mash it with a spoon to make sure there are no dry spots; if there are dry spots, add more buttermilk, 1 tablespoon at a time, until the bread is moist throughout.

Add the onion, garlic, Parmesan, parsley, salt, pepper, pancetta, egg yolk, oregano and demiglace to the bread-and-buttermilk mixture. Using a fork, mix everything together until it's thoroughly blended. Add the beef, veal and pork. Gently mix the meatball mixture by hand, teasing apart the ground meat with your fingers, just until everything is well combined. Avoid mixing any more than is necessary for everything to be evenly distributed. Using your hands, form the mixture into 24 golf ball–size meatballs.

1½ teaspoons kosher salt

¼ tablespoon freshly ground black pepper

2 ounces fatty pancetta, finely chopped

1 large egg yolk

1½ teaspoons fresh oregano, finely chopped

¼ cup homemade or store-bought veal demiglace

½ pound ground chuck

¼ pound ground short rib

½ pound ground veal

½ pound ground pork

2 tablespoons leaf lard (or vegetable oil)

For serving:

2 pounds dried rigatoni (or other pasta)

Freshly grated Parmesan cheese

Heat the leaf lard (or vegetable oil) in a large cast-iron skillet over medium-high heat. Working in batches, add the meatballs and sear on all sides. Add them to the sauce during its final hour of cooking. Alternatively, freeze them for up to 6 months.

Serve: Bring a large pot of salted water to a boil and cook the pasta until al dente. Drain the pasta and transfer it to a large serving bowl, then toss with enough sauce to coat it well. Top with the meatballs and more sauce. Sprinkle with Parmesan and serve.

"In prison, dinner was always a big thing. We had a pasta course and then we had a meat or a fish. Paulie did the prep work. He was doing a year for contempt, and he had this wonderful system for doing the garlic. He used a razor, and he used to slice it so thin that it used to liquefy in the pan with just a little oil. It's a very good system."

—Henry Hill

1990

★ PHILLY CHEESESTEAKS ★

In the *Rocky* quasi-sequel *Creed*, Adonis Johnson and his girlfriend-to-be, Bianca, treat themselves to greasy cheesesteaks on their first date. These famous Philadelphia sandwiches vary wildly from jawn to jawn, but follow the same basic formula: chewy roll, thinly sliced rib eye, cheese, and condiments. Controversially topped with ketchup and mayonnaise, this version strays slightly from what many Philadelphians would consider a proper cheesesteak. Follow the recipe below to the letter, or make it your own with American cheese, onions, Cheese Whiz, sautéed mushrooms, and/or tomatoes. Your exotic downstairs neighbor will thank you for it.

Ingredients

Makes 2 sandwiches

One 24-ounce boneless beef rib eye roast

1 teaspoon kosher salt

2 tablespoons vegetable oil

4 slices provolone cheese

Two 8-inch hoagie rolls, split

2 tablespoons ketchup

2 tablespoons mayonnaise

2 ounces sliced prepared sweet peppers or banana peppers

Season the rib eye all over with the salt and place on a wire rack set inside a rimmed baking sheet. Freeze for 30 minutes, or until firm to the touch. With a very sharp knife, slice the rib eye crosswise as thinly as possible, but do not trim any fat.

Heat the oil in two skillets (preferably cast iron) over medium-high heat until shimmering. Add half of the beef in an even layer to each skillet. Let the beef cook undisturbed until brown and crisp on the bottom, 2 to 3 minutes. Using a spatula, flip the meat and cook until it's well browned on the other side, about 2 minutes longer. Arrange the beef in an 8-inch-long pile in the center of each pan and top each pile with 2 slices of cheese. Lower the heat to medium low and cook until the cheese has melted.

Dress each roll with ketchup and mayonnaise. Place the bottom halves of the rolls on a plate, and, using a large spatula, transfer the beef from the skillets to the rolls. Top with peppers, add the top halves of the rolls and serve.

"Put extra peppers on that jawn, both kinds."
—*Bianca*

2015

★ POLLO A LA PLANCHA ★

Moonlight is the story of a young man's struggle growing up gay in one of Miami's roughest neighborhoods. The movie also happens to capitalize on the vibrancy of the city's local Latin American cuisine, using food as a metaphor for care and genuine intimacy. Pollo a la Plancha becomes a way for an old friend to nourish a broken man, and it's a great example of how simple ingredients become elevated when they're prepared with love.

Ingredients

Makes 4 servings

4 boneless skinless chicken breast halves

4 garlic cloves

4 limes

1 teaspoon ground cumin

1 teaspoon cayenne pepper

3 teaspoons kosher salt

1 teaspoon freshly ground black pepper

2 tablespoons olive oil

2 cups long-grain white rice

3½ cups plus ¼ cup water

1 bay leaf

4 ounces fatty bacon, finely chopped

2 medium Spanish onions, 1 finely chopped and 1 sliced into rings

1 green bell pepper, seeded and finely chopped

12 ounces dried black beans, soaked overnight

2 tablespoons vegetable oil

2 tablespoons chopped cilantro

> *"One chef's special...comin' right up."*
> *—Kevin*

Cut the chicken breasts in half lengthwise and pound with a meat hammer or small saucepan until evenly thick. Transfer the chicken to a large resealable bag. Roughly chop 2 of the garlic cloves. In a small bowl, whisk together the juice of 2 limes, the chopped garlic, cumin, cayenne, 1 teaspoon of salt, the black pepper and the olive oil. Pour the marinade over the chicken, seal the bag and refrigerate for at least 30 minutes.

In a large bowl, rinse the rice until the water runs clear. Drain the rice using a fine-mesh sieve, transfer to a large saucepan and cover with 3½ cups of water. Add the bay leaf, 1 teaspoon of salt and a garlic clove. Bring to a simmer over medium heat. Reduce the heat to low, cover the pot and cook for 15 minutes. Remove the pan from the heat and leave it covered. Let sit for 10 minutes, then fluff with a fork and keep warm until serving.

While the rice simmers, in a large saucepan combine the bacon and ¼ cup of water. Cook until the bacon fat has rendered and the bacon is crispy, about 5 to 7 minutes. Using a slotted spoon, remove the bacon and transfer it to a paper towel–lined plate. Add the chopped onion and green pepper to the reserved fat. Cook over medium heat until the vegetables have softened and the onion is golden brown, then add 1 crushed garlic clove. Cook until the garlic is fragrant, about 1 minute, then return the bacon to the pan and add the soaked black beans. Add enough water to just cover the beans, and bring the liquid to a simmer. Cook, uncovered, until the beans are tender and start to break apart and the liquid has thickened, about 1 hour. Season to taste with salt. Cover and keep warm until ready to serve.

On a cast-iron griddle or in a large cast-iron skillet, heat 1 tablespoon of vegetable oil over medium-high heat until shimmering. Add the sliced onion and cook, stirring occasionally, until lightly charred, about 2 minutes. Transfer the onion to a bowl and cover with aluminum foil until ready to serve.

Add the remaining tablespoon of vegetable oil to the griddle and heat over medium-high heat until shimmering. Remove the chicken from the marinade, shaking off any excess liquid, and place on the hot griddle. Cook the chicken until well browned on one side, about 5 minutes, then flip and cook until the other side is browned and the chicken is cooked through, about 5 minutes longer. Cut 1 of the remaining limes in half and squeeze both halves over the chicken.

Arrange the chicken, rice and beans on plates. Cut the remaining lime into quarters. Top the chicken with the sautéed onions, garnish with cilantro and the lime quarters and serve.

POPCORN WITH CHOCOLATE-COVERED RAISINS

Paul Reiser makes a thunderous comeback as Jim, the father of percussion prodigy Andrew Neiman, and teaches us all a foodie lesson: Popcorn tastes a million times better when you mix in some Raisinettes. Plunge your bloody hands into some ice water and whip up a batch of this concession stand mash-up to enjoy with your loving-but-skeptical father tonight. Just be sure to emotionally mislead an adoring young movie theater employee along the way.

Ingredients

Makes 2 large servings

8 ounces milk chocolate

1 cup raisins

⅓ cup coconut oil

½ cup popping corn

5 tablespoons butter, melted

1½ teaspoons kosher salt

In a double boiler, melt the chocolate over simmering water. (Alternatively, microwave the chocolate at 20 percent power for 15 seconds at a time, stirring between bursts, until melted). Remove from the heat, add the raisins and toss until the raisins are coated completely. Spread the raisins on a parchment-lined baking sheet. Transfer to the freezer and freeze until the coating has hardened, about 15 minutes. Break apart the raisins and let them return to room temperature.

In a large saucepan or Dutch oven, combine the coconut oil and 3 popcorn kernels. Cover the pot and heat over medium-high heat until you hear the kernels pop. Add the remaining popcorn, stir, lower the heat to medium and cover the pot. Cook the popcorn, occasionally swirling and shaking the pot, until all of the kernels have popped, about 2 to 3 minutes.

Pour the popcorn into a large bowl and drizzle with the melted butter while tossing to combine. Add the salt and toss again. Let the popcorn cool for 5 minutes before tossing with the chocolate covered raisins and serving.

2014

As far as burgers go, the Big Kahuna Burger is about as simple as they come: American cheese and a thin beef patty on a plain bun with a healthy slathering of ketchup. But watch the infamous "breakfast" scene from *Pulp Fiction* and try telling yourself that you don't need that burger, like right now. Maybe it's the idea of cheeseburgers for breakfast, maybe it's the idea of a fast food Hawaiian burger, maybe it's Jules's widening eyes as he tries his first bite that makes us so hungry— or maybe murder just works up an appetite.

OSCAR-WORTHY
FOOD PERFORMANCE

No. 3

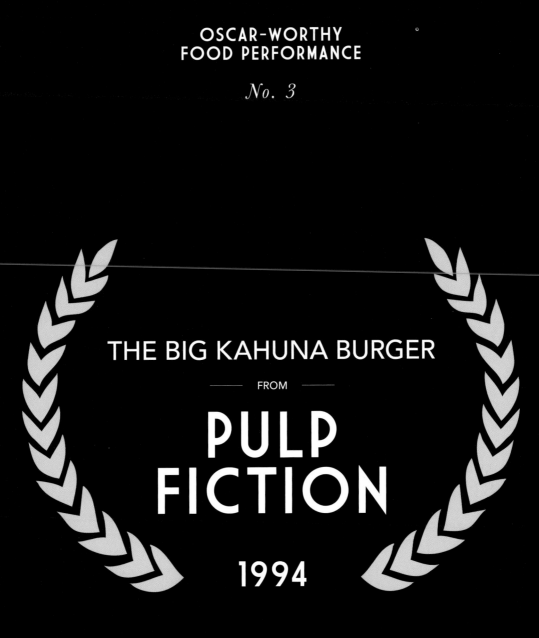

THE BIG KAHUNA BURGER

— FROM —

PULP FICTION

1994

★ SHRIMP COCKTAIL ★

Tim Burton's fantastical gothic tales are often peppered with fanciful and cartoonish foodstuffs, and the shrimp cocktail that appears in his seminal classic *Beetlejuice* is no exception. Considering the fact they're being served at a haunted dinner where ghostly inhabitants of an old house try to scare away their human successors (oh, and they ultimately become face-grabbing hands after a Harry Belafonte–backed dance sequence), these shrimp cocktails actually look fresh and delectable on screen—as does Catherine O'Hara.

Ingredients

Makes 4 servings

1 lemon, halved

1 leek (white and light green parts)—trimmed, halved lengthwise and rinsed

1 bay leaf

1 medium carrot, halved crosswise

1 rib celery, halved crosswise

1 head garlic, halved widthwise

1 tablespoon black peppercorns

5 parsley sprigs

3 thyme sprigs

2 quarts water

24 jumbo shell-on shrimp

1 cup ketchup

¼ cup prepared horseradish

1 teaspoon Tabasco

½ teaspoon Worcestershire sauce

In a stockpot, combine half of the lemon, the leek, bay leaf, carrot, celery, garlic, peppercorns, parsley and thyme with 2 quarts of water. Bring to a simmer, cover and cook for 30 minutes. Add the shrimp, turn off the heat and let the shrimp cook until they're bright pink and cooked through, about 2 to 4 minutes, depending on their size. Remove the shrimp, then peel and devein, leaving the tails intact. Transfer them to a bowl, cover with plastic wrap and refrigerate until ready to serve.

In a medium bowl, stir together the ketchup, horseradish, Tabasco and Worcestershire sauce until well mixed. Arrange the shrimp around a serving bowl filled with cocktail sauce (or several small, sauce-filled bowls or cocktail glasses) and serve.

"It's showtime!"

—*Beetlejuice*

1988

★ STEAMED AND ROASTED DUCK ★

The Taiwanese film *Eat Drink Man Woman* opens with a memorable food scene: a master chef demonstrates an impressive range of cooking skills in his home kitchen to the audience's drooling wonderment. Life in this family, which consists of the chef and his three adult daughters, revolves around the sacred ritual of Sunday dinner, where a feast of duck meat is prepared and served without exception. Even if you aren't raising fresh fowl in your backyard, or can't make short work of a mountain of vegetables with your Damascus Nakiri knife, you can still experience some of the smells and flavors that Mr. Chu and his daughters enjoyed every Sunday.

Ingredients

Makes 4 servings

One 5-pound whole Pekin duck

2 tablespoons sugar

¼ cup soy sauce

2 tablespoons hoisin sauce

1½ teaspoons fish sauce

1 clove garlic, finely chopped

1½ teaspoons honey

½ teaspoon salt

½ teaspoon freshly ground black pepper

½ teaspoon ground star anise

Steamed rice, for serving

Place the duck, breast side down, on a cutting board. Use kitchen shears or a serrated knife to remove the duck's spine, making sure not to cut into the thigh. Press down on the bird to flatten it. Remove any extra pockets of fat.

Place a wire rack inside a roasting pan or casserole and set the duck, breast side up, inside. In a small bowl, whisk together the sugar, soy sauce, hoisin sauce, fish sauce, garlic, honey, salt, pepper and star anise and brush all over the duck. Refrigerate for at least 2 hours.

Preheat the oven to 350°. Brush the duck with the glaze again and add about ½ inch of water to the bottom of the pan. Cover the pan with aluminum foil, leaving some room above the duck but sealing the sides tightly in order to trap steam. Roast for 1 hour, then remove the foil, brush the duck with glaze and roast, uncovered, until an instant-read thermometer inserted into the thickest part of the thigh reaches 165°. If the skin isn't brown enough, preheat the broiler, then broil the duck until the skin is dark and crispy.

Transfer the duck to a cutting board. Using a fine-mesh sieve, strain the liquid from the roasting pan into a saucepan. Bring the liquid to a boil and reduce until it's syrupy. Carve the duck and transfer the pieces to a serving platter. Pour the sauce over the duck and serve with steamed rice.

"I cannot live my life
like my methods of cooking."
—*Chu*

1994

★ IL TIMPANO ★

If *Big Night* is the sacred church of film food fandom, then Il Timpano is its sacrament. A decadent, laborious centerpiece suited for a large dinner party, this towering Italian showstopper sends Ian Holm's character into an over-the-top demonstration of anger-filled ecstasy. The dish features handmade garganelli pasta, meatballs, soppressata, hard-boiled eggs, two kinds of cheese, and a slow-simmered sauce, so you may want to set aside an entire weekend for the Timpano challenge. Just be sure to avoid the Stanley Tucci blunder of inviting both of your lovers to the same party.

Ingredients

Makes 12 servings

For the garganelli:

10 ounces Tipo "00" flour (or all-purpose flour), plus more for dusting

2 whole large eggs plus 4 egg yolks

1 teaspoon kosher salt

For the timpano dough:

15 ounces Tipo "00" flour, plus more for dusting

2 whole large eggs plus 6 egg yolks

2 tablespoons olive oil

2 teaspoons kosher salt

For the timpano:

2 tablespoons olive oil

3 cups Prison Gravy (see page 90)

8 hard-boiled eggs, halved lengthwise

24 meatballs (see page 90)

½ pound grated aged provolone

1 pound low moisture mozzarella, cut into 1-inch cubes

¾ pound soppressata, sliced into ⅛-inch rounds

1 egg, beaten

Whole nutmeg, for grating

Make the garganelli: On a wood surface or a silicone baking mat, form the flour into a mound with a well in the center large enough to hold the eggs. Pour the eggs and salt into the well and beat with a fork, slowly adding more and more flour, until a thick slurry is formed. Begin working in the flour with your hands to form a shaggy dough. Knead for 5 minutes, until the dough is smooth and elastic. Wrap in plastic wrap and let rest for 30 minutes.

Using a bench scraper, divide the dough into six pieces of equal size. Roll the pieces, one at a time (keep the remaining pieces covered with plastic wrap), into a rectangular shape on a well-floured surface until they are thin enough so that you can see the outline of your hand through the dough. Using a pizza or pasta cutter, cut the edges off the rolled-out dough to form a rectangle. Cut the rectangle into 2-inch squares, wrap diagonally around a small wooden dowel and press against a gnocchi striper to form garganelli. Place the pasta pieces on a floured, towel-lined baking sheet, leaving space between them, and let dry overnight before preparing the timpano.

Make the timpano dough: On a wood surface or a silicone baking mat, form the flour into a mound with a well in the center large enough to hold the eggs. Pour the eggs, oil and salt into the well and beat with a fork, slowly adding more and more flour, until a thick slurry is formed. Begin working in the flour with your hands to form a shaggy dough. Knead for 5 minutes, until the dough is smooth and not tacky. (If the dough starts to spring back as you knead, cover it with a kitchen towel and let rest for a few minutes before continuing to roll out.) Wrap the dough in plastic wrap and let rest for 30 minutes.

Unwrap the dough and dust it with flour. On a well-floured work surface, roll it out into a large circle, dusting with flour as needed, until it's about ⅛-inch thick.

Assemble the timpano: Preheat the oven to 375°.

Coat the interior of a 5-quart enameled Dutch oven with oil. Transfer the timpano dough to the Dutch oven by loosely rolling it around the rolling pin, then unrolling it over the pot. Line the pot with the dough, pressing it into the seams, leaving about 8 inches of dough hanging over the side.

Bring a large saucepan of water to a boil and cook the garganelli until almost al dente. Drain it and transfer to a bowl. Toss the garganelli with enough gravy to keep it from sticking together, about 1 cup.

Fill the dough-lined Dutch oven with a layer of pasta and sauce mixture (about ¼ of the total amount). Begin forming layers using ¼ of each of the fillings: hard-boiled eggs, meatballs, cheeses, salami, and gravy. Repeat until timpano is filled to the brim. Finish with a layer of provolone to help prevent the ingredients from leaking after the timpano is flipped over. Fold the excess dough over the top and press down to seal. Brush the dough with the beaten egg. For a softer crust, cover the Dutch oven and bake for about 2 hours, until the dough is golden brown and an instant-read thermometer inserted into the middle of the timpano registers 125°. For a crisper crust, bake uncovered.

When done, let the timpano rest for one hour in the Dutch oven. Then run a pairing knife around the edge of it to loosen the sides (be careful not to slice into the dough). Place a cutting board or a platter over the top of the Dutch oven and invert the timpano onto it. Cut it into wedges and serve over a pool of warm gravy. Grate some nutmeg over the top and serve.

"GOD DAMN IT!

God damn it I should kill you...it's so

fucking good, I should kill you."

—Pascal

The be-all and end-all of Italian mobster movies has the be-all and end-all of red sauces: the prison gravy. Vinnie's prison time not only offers a fascinating look at the real-life incarceration of Henry Hill, but it also depicts a positively classic Italian red sauce. We can almost hear its quiet simmer, smell its garlicky aroma, taste its unmistakable flavor. It makes us wish we were in that luxurious prision with him. Wine and prosciutto just seem as though they'd taste so much sweeter if they were smuggled to us in a laundry bag by a crooked prison guard.

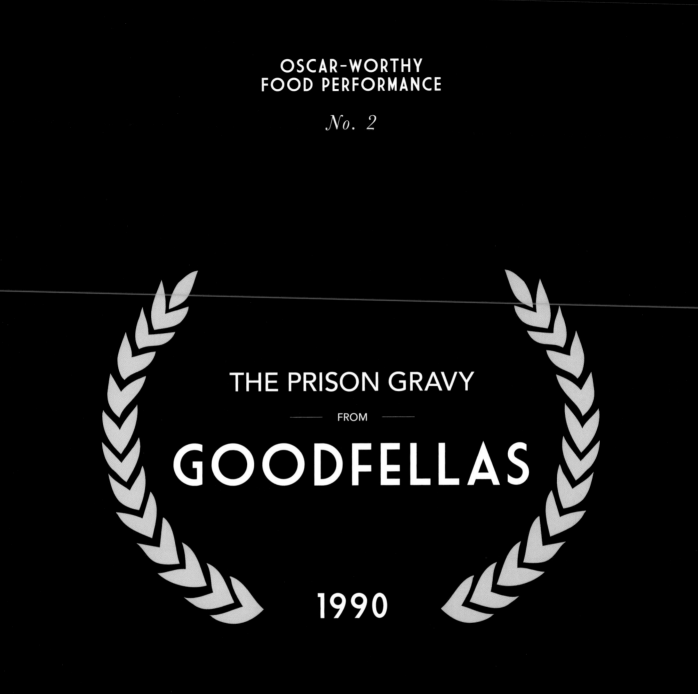

OSCAR-WORTHY
FOOD PERFORMANCE

No. 2

THE PRISON GRAVY

— FROM —

GOODFELLAS

1990

★ TIRAMISU ★

In what may be the last great high school gross-out comedy, tiramisu is the assignment du jour in Jonah Hill and Emma Stone's home economics class. Lewd gestures and flour face paint aside, the final results look surprisingly tasty. Although the students make ladyfingers from scratch, I find that some things are just better store-bought. Make sure to keep extra cocoa and chocolate shavings on hand to cover up potential imperfections when you're assembling the layers.

Ingredients

Makes 8 servings

6 large egg yolks

½ cup sugar

2 cups heavy whipping cream

2 cups mascarpone cheese, at room temperature

1 cup brewed espresso, cooled

¼ cup Cognac

32 ladyfingers

Cocoa powder, for dusting

4 ounces dark chocolate, shaved

In a large bowl, whisk together the egg yolks and sugar until pale. In a saucepan, bring 1 cup of cream to just under a boil. While whisking the egg yolks, slowly pour in the hot cream. Pour the mixture back into the saucepan, whisking over low heat until thick enough to coat the back of a spoon. Remove from the heat and let cool.

In a bowl, whip the remaining cup of cream until soft peaks form. Fold the mascarpone into the cooled egg yolk–cream mixture, then fold in the whipped cream.

In a small bowl, whisk together the espresso and Cognac. Quickly dip the ladyfingers in the coffee mixture (don't let them soak up too much liquid). Line the bottom of a 9-by-13-inch casserole with a layer of ladyfingers and spread half of the custard evenly over the top. Top with another layer of ladyfingers and another layer of custard. Cover with plastic wrap and refrigerate for at least 3 hours.

Just before serving, dust the top of the tiramisu with cocoa powder. Cut into squares, garnish each piece with shaved dark chocolate and serve.

"I don't wanna sit here all by myself cooking this shitty food, no offense, and I just think that I don't ever need to cook tiramisu. When am I gonna need to cook tiramisu? Am I gonna be a chef? No. There's three weeks left of school—gimme a fucking break."

—Seth

2007

★ TONKOTSU RAMEN ★

For most Westerners, ramen conjures up images of instant noodles hastily consumed in college dorm rooms after midnight. But any fan of Japanese cuisine will tell you that ramen is a complex dish worthy of respect and appreciation. To quote the ramen master from the 1985 movie *Tampopo*: "First, observe the whole bowl. Appreciate its gestalt, savor the aromas." Watching Ken Watanabe learn how to properly eat ramen might give you enough of a craving to try to make your own version of tonkotsu ramen from scratch.

Ingredients

Makes 4 servings

5 pounds pig trotters, sliced into 2-inch-thick rounds, rinsed and scrubbed

½ pound pork fatback

1 large onion, quartered

One 3-pound piece of pork belly

½ cup soy sauce

½ cup mirin or white wine

½ cup chicken stock

1 tablespoon fish sauce

1 tablespoon miso paste

1 pound fresh ramen noodles

1 package *naruto* (Japanese fish cake), sliced

4 sheets of *nori*

1 pound enoki mushrooms, cleaned and separated

4 scallions, sliced into rings

Make the tonkotsu broth: In a large stockpot, cover the pig trotters with cold water and bring to a boil for 5 minutes. Drain the trotters and rinse under cold water. Scrub any scum off the bones, then put them back in the stockpot and cover with cold water again. Add the fatback and onion to the pot and bring the contents to a boil. Reduce the heat to medium low, cover and cook at a gentle boil (more than a simmer) for 12 to 18 hours, or until the broth is fatty and milky. Strain the broth through a cheesecloth-lined sieve and discard the solids; reserve the fatback. Refrigerate the broth until ready to serve (you should have about 6 quarts).

Roll the pork belly into a log and tie with butcher twine. Place the belly in a large resealable bag. In a bowl, whisk together the soy sauce, mirin (or wine), stock, fish sauce and miso paste. Add the marinade to the bag, seal the bag and refrigerate for 4 hours.

Preheat the oven to 300°. Place the pork belly in a large loaf pan or small baking dish with enough marinade to reach halfway up the side of the pork. Transfer the pan to the oven and braise for about 3 hours, or the pork is tender. Remove the pan from the oven and let cool for 30 to 60 minutes before covering with plastic wrap. Refrigerate until ready to serve.

Assemble the ramen: In a large saucepan, bring the tonkotsu broth to a simmer. Finely chop the fatback and add to the broth, simmering until it's barely visible in the broth. Ladle the broth into wide bowls, leaving room for the noodles and toppings. (Freeze any leftover broth to use later.) Cook the noodles according to the package instructions and divide among bowls. Top each with 2 slices of pork belly, 3 slices of *naruto*, 1 sheet of *nori*, the enoki mushrooms and scallions. Serve immediately.

"What's important here is to apologize to the pork by saying 'see you soon.'"
—Ramen Master

1985

TAMPOPO

★ VANILLA BEAN CRÈME BRÛLÉE ★

Amélie, a French film with elements of magical realism, features a quirky leading lady who teaches us how to enjoy the little pleasures in life: the oddly satisfying feeling of sticking your hand in a bagful of green lentils, hearing the plop of a stone skipped at precisely the right angle—and the unmistakable crack of a crème brûlée's sugary crust being shattered with a spoon. This surprisingly easy dessert is sure to impress, and you too will revel in the satisfying crunch and creamy interior of a perfectly executed brûlée.

Ingredients

Makes 4 servings

6 large egg yolks

½ cup granulated sugar

2½ cups heavy cream

1 vanilla bean, split and scraped

¼ cup turbinado sugar

In a small bowl, beat the egg yolks and granulated sugar together until the sugar has dissolved and the yolks grow slightly pale. Set aside.

In a saucepan, bring the cream and vanilla bean scrapings and pod to a boil. Lower the heat and gently simmer for 5 minutes. Remove the pan from the heat, discard the vanilla bean pod and let the cream cool for 10 minutes. Whisking constantly, slowly pour the cream into the egg-sugar mixture. In a saucepan bring 1 inch of water to a simmer. Place the bowl with the cream-egg mixture over the saucepan. Cook the custard, whisking constantly, until thick enough to coat the back of a spoon.

Line the bottom of a baking pan or other high-walled ovenproof dish with paper towels and place 4 large ramekins or crème brûlée dishes inside. Carefully pour the mixture into the ramekins, leaving about ½ inch of room at the top. Pour enough boiling water into the baking pan to reach halfway up the sides of the ramekins. Carefully place the pan in the oven and bake for 40 to 50 minutes, or until the custard is set but jiggles in the center. Remove the ramekins from the pan and refrigerate until completely cooled, at least 90 minutes.

Sprinkle turbinado sugar evenly over the tops of the crème brûlées. Using a blow torch (or broiler), caramelize the sugar until browned. Serve immediately.

"Instead she cultivates a taste for small pleasures: putting her hand in a bag of seeds, piercing the crust of a crème brûlée with a spoon."

2001

★ VIENNESE STRUDEL ★

In one of cinema's most terrifying food scenes, Nazi Colonel Hans Landa (played by Christoph Waltz) toys with a young Jewish cinema proprietor, Shosanna, using thinly veiled threats over a piece of apple strudel. Never before has whipped cream or a glass of milk carried such dramatic tension, but despite the stomach-churning anxiety we can read on Shosanna's face, it's hard not to want a bite of the flaky Austrian treat the Nazi sociopath eats. Your experience making and enjoying this strudel will almost certainly be more palatable.

Ingredients

Makes 8 servings

1½ cups bread flour, plus more for dusting, sprinkling and filling

¼ cup vegetable oil, plus more for the dough

1 large egg, beaten, plus 2 egg whites

½ teaspoon kosher salt

Zest of 1 lemon plus 1½ teaspoons fresh lemon juice

¼ cup warm water (about 110°)

3 baking apples, peeled and sliced thinly

½ cup plus 1 tablespoon granulated sugar

½ cup raisins

1 tablespoon ground cinnamon

1 stick unsalted butter, melted

½ cup finely chopped walnuts, hazelnuts or almonds

1 cup heavy cream

Confectioners' sugar, for garnish

"Wait for the cream"
—Hans Landa

Place the flour in a large bowl and create a well in the center with your fingers. Fill the well with the oil, 2 egg whites, salt and lemon juice. Mix with your fingers until just combined and sprinkle with the water. Knead until a shaggy dough forms. Turn the dough out onto a lightly floured tabletop and knead vigorously, until the dough is soft and supple, about 5 to 7 minutes. Place in a lightly oiled bowl and let rest for 30 minutes.

In a bowl, toss the apples with ½ cup of granulated sugar, lemon zest, raisins and cinnamon, and set aside.

Cover a large work surface with a clean cotton sheet or tablecloth and liberally dust with flour. Roll the dough out on the tablecloth until it forms a circle about 24 inches in diameter. Using floured fists, lift the dough and stretch it out as large as possible without tearing. If the dough starts to spring back, cover it with a towel and let rest for a few minutes before continuing to roll out. Place the dough on the cloth and gently tug at its edges until it's thin enough to see through. Trim the edges of the dough to form a large rectangle. Brush the dough with the melted butter until evenly coated. Sprinkle evenly with the chopped nuts.

Preheat the oven to 375°. Place the apple mixture on one side of the dough rectangle. Using the tablecloth, fold the end of the dough with the apples over, brushing the newly exposed dough covering the apples with melted butter. Repeat until the apples are at the center of a long roll. Pinch the ends together to seal the contents in and place the dough, seam side down, on a parchment paper–lined baking sheet. Brush the pastry liberally with the beaten egg.

Bake the strudel for 40 to 50 minutes, basting with melted butter every 10 minutes or so, until golden brown. Let cool at least 1 hour before slicing.

In a bowl, beat the cream and remaining 1 tablespoon of granulated sugar to stiff peaks. Slice the strudel and dust with confectioners' sugar. Spoon a large dollop of whipped cream onto each slice and serve.

INSPIRED BY

WORLD'S GREATEST SANDWICH

In addition to *Ratatouille* (page 52), American culinary legend Thomas Keller also served as a food consultant for *Spanglish*, the film your aunt insisted was a "must-see." It might not have wowed at the box office, but it made our stomachs grumble as a more-serious-than-usual Adam Sandler took a chef's approach to a midnight snack. What could have been just another BLT was perfected with an oozing, runny fried egg. Enjoy with a tall beer for maximum happiness.

Ingredients

Makes 1 sandwich

4 slices thick-cut bacon

1 whole egg plus 2 egg yolks

1 teaspoon Dijon mustard

Juice of 1 lemon

½ cup vegetable oil

Kosher salt

2 slices pain de campagne or other country bread

½ cup (about 2 ounces) grated Monterey Jack cheese

1 beefsteak tomato, sliced

2 leaves butter lettuce

Preheat the oven to 350°. Set a wire rack inside a rimmed baking sheet and arrange the bacon on top. Bake for 20 to 25 minutes, or until crisp. Transfer the bacon to a paper towel–lined plate, reserving the fat from the baking sheet.

Make the mayonnsaise: Place the egg yolks in a blender along with the mustard, lemon juice, ¼ cup of oil and a ½ teaspoon of salt. Pulse until combined. With the blender running at low speed, slowly add the remaining ¼ cup of oil, blending until the mayonnaise is thick and creamy.

In a small nonstick skillet, heat the reserved bacon fat over medium heat until shimmering. Add the whole egg and fry until the white is set but the yolk is still runny.

Top 1 slice of bread with the grated cheese and toast in the oven until the cheese has melted and the bread is crisp. Toast the other slice of bread, and spread the mayonnaise on one side. Top with the tomato slices and sprinkle with a pinch of salt. Top with the butter lettuce, bacon and the sunny-side up egg. Assemble the sandwich, cut it in half and serve.

2004

INSPIRED BY

SPANGLISH

The culinary payoff in a small, quiet film about a pair of Italian brothers in 1950s New Jersey is one for the books, and any Top 10 list would be incomplete without this Louis Prima fete. With dishes ranging from familiar to fascinating, it's a meditation on food as an event, a unifier and an expression of fraternity. Despite the fact that their guest of honor never arrives, brother restaurateurs Primo and Secondo exercise no restraint. They lavish course after course upon their delighted guests despite knowing that it may be the last meal their restaurant serves. They are, first and foremost, passionate about food—its ability to widen perspectives, charm palates and gather friends and foes. "My mother was a terrible cook," a patron sobs into the empty plates after the meal concludes. It's a throwaway joke in the script, but it's also the reason why *Big Night* is the greatest food film of all time: It's all about the importance of food.

ALL THE FOOD

— FROM —

BIG NIGHT

1996

This book would not have been possible, first and foremost, without the hard work, patience and creativity of the people at Dovetail Press. A special thanks is also warmly extended to Olivia Anderson, who tirelessly tested the recipes to make sure I didn't mess it up too badly.

Since I was old enough to hold a camera, my dad has been a constant source of wisdom and inspiration. The closer we've become over the years, the more I find myself branching out, pushing hard, taking risks. Any future success I have is owed to him. My brother David, when he's not giving me some much-needed grounding, lifts me up with encouragement and inspires me with his successes as an engineer, husband and father. His son (my nephew) Christopher is my biggest fan, and I'm excited to see what bright future lies ahead of him, surrounded by so many gifted and loving people. I'm also forever grateful to my wonderful family for their constant love and support: Barb, Kelly, Donna, Lauren, Josh, Kathy and Bob.

My employers of more than seven years (and dear friends), Diana Dayrit and Jon Magel, are also owed a huge debt of gratitude—not only for looking the other way when I was writing during work hours, but also for endlessly supporting every cockeyed idea and crazy pipe dream I ever had, even as those pursuits slowly stole me away from their company. I wouldn't be the person I am today without them.

I'm privileged to have a small circle of impossibly close friends, all of whom have played a hand in cultivating my values and priorities, especially Sawyer Jacobs for his unbridled creativity, humor and warmth, and Rashid Duroseau for his limitless intelligence, kindness and patience with my destroying our kitchen. To Doug Balkin, Max Carithers, Jon Allen, Rob Meade, Steven Farrell and Eddie Liu: You've been there for me through the years with advice, encouragement and enduring friendship that I'll forever cherish and reciprocate.

Last (but certainly not least) is the person who changed my life forever, opened my eyes to new ideas, gave me newfound courage and confidence and convinced me that I have a voice. We were brought together by impossible circumstances and have already surmounted impossible obstacles. Katie, life is so much bigger with you in it, and I've never been so excited to see what comes next. You constantly inspire, enrich and enliven me. I love you madly.

About the Author

Andrew Rea is one part chef, one part filmmaker and a generous dash of irreverent YouTube personality. Self-taught both behind and in front of the camera, Andrew created his cooking show, *Binging with Babish* in 2016. Millions of burgeoning chefs and foodies around the globe now enjoy the series. His passion for teaching and experimenting in the kitchen is rivaled only by his love of film and television, both of which he endeavors to share from his Harlem, New York, kitchen.

CREDITS

PHOTOGRAPHY — SCOTT GORDON BLEICHER

BOOK DESIGN — WILL PAY

SET DESIGN AND PROP STYLING — BEN KNOX & CHRISTOPHER SPAULDING OF RECLAIM DESIGN, (RCDNYC.COM)

RECIPE TESTING FOOD STYLING — OLIVIA MACK ANDERSON

COPY EDITOR — ABBY TANNENBAUM

PRODUCTION ASSISTANT — MAPLETHORPE KELLY

MODELS — ADAM DANKER-FELDMAN
NICK FAUCHALD
MAY HEIN
ADITI KUMAR
CARLO MANTUANO
JEREMY PETERS
ELIZABETH TILTON

AND A SPECIAL THANKS TO:
AMBER & SEBASTIAN COTTRELL, ROB SHMALO, APRIL JAMES, THE HOODRATZ, FISHS EDDY

INDEX

CREDITS

PHOTOGRAPHY	SCOTT GORDON BLEICHER
BOOK DESIGN	WILL PAY
SET DESIGN AND PROP STYLING	BEN KNOX & CHRISTOPHER SPAULDING OF RECLAIM DESIGN. (RCDNYC.COM)
RECIPE TESTING FOOD STYLING	OLIVIA MACK ANDERSON
COPY EDITOR	ABBY TANNENBAUM
PRODUCTION ASSISTANT	MAPLETHORPE KELLY
MODELS	ADAM DANKER-FELDMAN
	NICK FAUCHALD
	MAY HEIN
	ADITI KUMAR
	CARLO MANTUANO
	JEREMY PETERS
	ELIZABETH TILTON

AND A SPECIAL THANKS TO:
AMBER & SEBASTIAN COTTRELL, ROB SHMALO, APRIL JAMES, THE HOODRATZ, FISHS EDDY

INDEX

A DOVETAIL PRODUCTION
MMXVII

DOVETAIL

Text copyright © 2017 by Andrew Rea

Photographs © 2017 by Scott Gordon Bleicher

Design by Will Pay

Published by Dovetail Press in Brooklyn, New York, a division of Assembly Brands LLC.

For details or ordering information, contact the publisher at the address below or email info@dovetail.press.

Dovetail Press

42 West Street #403

Brooklyn, NY 11222

www.dovetail.press

Library of Congress Cataloging-in-Publication data is on file with the publisher.

ISBN: 978-0-9987399-5-3

First Edition

Printed in the USA

10 9 8 7 6 5 4 3 2